AN INTRODUCTION TO
Sets, Groups, and Matrices

AN INTRODUCTION TO
Sets, Groups, and Matrices

A. BALFOUR, M.A., F.I.M.A., F.B.C.S.

Professor of Computer Science
Heriot-Watt University, Edinburgh

SECOND EDITION

HEINEMANN EDUCATIONAL BOOKS
LONDON

Heinemann Educational Books Ltd

LONDON EDINBURGH MELBOURNE AUCKLAND TORONTO
SINGAPORE HONG KONG KUALA LUMPUR
IBADAN NAIROBI JOHANNESBURG
LUSAKA NEW DELHI

ISBN 0 435 51060 6

© A. Balfour 1965, 1966

First published 1965
Second edition 1966
Reprinted 1970, 1974

Published by
Heinemann Educational Books Ltd
48 Charles Street, London W1X 8AH
Reproduced and printed by photolithography and bound in
Great Britain at The Pitman Press, Bath

PREFACE

This book has been written with the needs in mind of fifth and sixth year secondary and grammar school pupils who have previously followed a traditional O-level course in mathematics. The two main chapters of the book are concerned with the algebra of sets and the algebra of matrices respectively, and the remaining chapters cover, in much less detail, some introductory aspects of binary operations and the theory of groups. University and Technical College students will also find the work of value as a brief introduction to these topics.

My sincere thanks are due to Mr. J. J. Armstrong, Heriot-Watt University, Mr. A. W. Campbell, George Heriot's School, and Mr. W. Craig, Daniel Stewart's College, who have assisted me considerably in the development of the text. My thanks are also due to Mrs. R. Brown, Heriot-Watt University, who prepared the typed version of the manuscript, and finally to Mr. H. MacGibbon, Heinemann Educational Books Ltd. Without his enthusiastic help and guidance, the transition from manuscript form to final printed version could not have been achieved in such a smooth manner.

Heriot-Watt University   A.B.
December 1964.

PREFACE TO SECOND EDITION

The first edition of this text has been augmented by the addition of a chapter covering some topics of the algebra of propositions. A few other minor amendments have also been made.

Heriot-Watt University   A.B.
February 1966.

CONTENTS

Chapter One

BASIC SET THEORY

1.1 *Introduction*

The idea of a *set* (or *class*) of objects is a familiar one in mathematics and in every-day life.

Example 1 The books in a library constitute a set, the *members* (or *elements*) of this set being the individual books in the library.

Example 2 The prime numbers 1, 2, 3, 5, 7, 11, . . . constitute a set and each prime number is an element of this set.

No attempt will be made to give a precise definition of the words 'element' and 'set' but it will be assumed that, given a set A and an element x, it is possible to decide whether or not x is an element of the set A.

1.2 *Notation*

We will use A, B, C, D, E, . . . to denote sets and a, b, c, d, e, . . . to denote elements. We will write $m \in X$ if m is an element of the set X, and $m \notin X$ if m is not an element of the set X. The symbolic statement $m \in X$ is usually read 'm is an element of the set X.'

Example 1 If A is the set of all even integers then $2 \in A$ but $7 \notin A$.

When a set is specified by listing the elements a, b, c, . . . contained in it we will write

$$A = \{a, b, c, . . .\}$$

and we will speak of the set a, b, c, . . .

Example 2 A = {1, 2, 3, 4} indicates that A is the set with elements 1, 2, 3 and 4.

Example 3 X = {a, b, e} indicates that X is the set with elements a, b and e.

Example 4 P = {1, 2, 3, 5, 7, 11, . . .} indicates that P is the set of all prime numbers.

Example 5 A = {{1, 2}, {1, 3}, {2, 3}} indicates that A is the set whose elements are the sets {1, 2}, {1, 3} and {2, 3}.

A set may also be specified by the 'defining property' method, i.e. by stating the requirements which an element must satisfy to belong to the set. The symbol : will be used for 'such that' as indicated in the following examples.

Example 6 P = {x : x is a prime number} indicates that P is the set of all elements x such that x is a prime number, i.e. P is the set of all prime numbers.

Example 7 A = {x : x² − 3x + 2 = 0} indicates that A is the set of all elements x such that $x^2 - 3x + 2 = 0$, i.e. A = {1, 2}.

EXERCISES 1.2

1. List the elements contained in the following sets, given that N is the set of positive integers and P is the set of all prime numbers.

(a) A = {x : x² = 25}

(b) H = {x : 3x + 2 = 0 or 2x + 3 = 0}

(c) G = {x : x² − 4x + 3 = 0 and 2x² − 3x + 1 = 0}

(d) B = {x : x ∈ N and x is even}

(e) F = {x : x ∈ P and x is divisible by 3}

(f) C = {x : x ∈ N and x ∉ P}

1.3 Set Inclusion and the Equality of Sets

We will say that the set A is 'contained' in the set B, and write A ⊂ B, if and only if every element of the set A is also an element of set B. We will also say that A is a *subset* of B, and if, in addition, there is at least one element of B, which is not an element of A, then we will say that A is a *proper subset* of B.

Example 1 If A = {1, 3, 4,} and B = {1, 2, 3, 4, 5, 6} then A is a proper subset of B and we may write A ⊂ B.

Example 2 If X = {1, 3} and Y = {$x : x^2 - 4x + 3 = 0$} then X is a subset of Y and we may write X ⊂ Y. Note that X is not a proper subset of Y.

We will also say that the set A is *equal* to the set B, and write A = B, if and only if the two sets contain exactly the same elements. It immediately follows that one method of showing the equality of two sets, say X and Y, is to show that X ⊂ Y and Y ⊂ X. This technique will be exploited later.

Example 3 If A = {1, 2, 3} and B = {3, 1, 2} then A = B.

Example 4 If A = {1, 2, 3, 5} and B = {$x : x$ is a prime number and $x < 6$} then A = B.

EXERCISES 1.3

1. Examine the following statements and decide whether each statement is true or false.

$$(a)\ x \in \{x, y, z\} \qquad (b)\ x \subset \{x, y, z\}$$
$$(c)\ \{x\} \in \{x, y, z\} \qquad (d)\ \{x\} \subset \{x, y, z\}$$

2. Let C be the set of all cyclic quadrilaterals,
  P be the set of all parallelograms,
  Q be the set of all quadrilaterals,
  R be the set of all rectangles,
  S be the set of all squares,
  T be the set of all trapezia,
  V be the set of all rhombuses,

Which of the following are correct?

(a) S ⊂ R (b) V ⊂ P

(c) R ⊂ P ⊂ Q (d) T ⊂ P

(e) S ⊂ R ⊂ P ⊂ T ⊂ Q (f) T ⊂ C ⊂ Q

1.4 *Special Sets*

The set containing all elements under discussion in a particular problem is called the *universal* set and is denoted by the symbol $\mathscr{E}$. Note that the universal set changes from problem to problem.
The set containing *no* elements is called the *null* set and is denoted by the symbol ϕ. Note that, by definition, ϕ is a subset of every set. It is also important to note that ϕ and $\mathscr{E}$, as used here, are not numbers, but the symbols for special sets.

Example 1 ϕ and $\{\phi\}$ are quite different. ϕ is the null set and $\{\phi\}$ is the set containing the one element ϕ.

Example 2   List all the subsets of the set $\{a, b, c\}$. How many of these subsets are proper subsets?
The required subsets are

$$\{a, b, c\}, \quad \{a, b\}, \quad \{a, c\}, \quad \{b, c\},$$

$$\{a\}, \quad \{b\}, \quad \{c\}, \quad \phi.$$

Seven of these subsets are proper subsets, the exception being $\{a, b, c\}$.

Example 3*   How many subsets has a set which contains n elements?
Subsets can be formed by selecting $0, 1, 2, 3, \ldots, n$ elements belonging to the given set.

Hence NO. of subsets $= {}^nC_0 + {}^nC_1 + {}^nC_2 + \ldots + {}^nC_n$

$$= 2^n.$$

Alternatively, we can think of a subset being constructed by examining each of the n elements in turn and either retaining it or rejecting it. Hence there are $2 \times 2 \times 2 \times 2 \ldots \times 2 = 2^n$ possible subsets.
Given a set A, then the set which contains all the elements of the universal set, which are *not* elements of A, is called the *complement* of A, and is denoted by A$'$. Thus

$$A' = \{x : x \in \mathscr{E} \text{ and } x \notin A\}$$

* An asterisk attached to any example or exercise indicates that the result of the piece of work is of importance and worth remembering.

Example 4 If the universal set is the set of all integers and
A = {x:x is an even integer}, then A′ = {x:x is an odd integer}.

Example 5 What is the complement of ϕ and of $\mathcal{E}$?
By definition $\phi' = \mathcal{E}$ and $\mathcal{E}' = \phi$.

1.5 Combinations of Sets

Given two sets A and B, we define the *union of A and B* to be
that set consisting of all elements which are elements of either
A or B, or both, and we write it A ∪ B.

Given two sets A and B, we define the *intersection of A and B*
to be that set consisting of all elements which are elements of
both A and B, and we write it A ∩ B.

Thus   A ∪ B = {x:x ∈ A *or* x ∈ B, or both}

A ∩ B = {x:x ∈ A *and* x ∈ B}

Note that A ∪ B is read as 'A plus B' or 'A or B' or 'A cup B'
whereas A ∩ B is read as 'A times B' or 'A and B' or 'A cap B.'
Note also that if $x \in A$ or $x \in B$ then $x \in A \cup B$, and if $x \in A$
and $x \in B$ then $x \in A \cap B$. The converse statements also hold.

Example 1 If A = {1, 2, 3, 4, 5} and B = {2, 4, 6, 8} then
A ∪ B = {1, 2, 3, 4, 5, 6, 8} and A ∩ B = {2, 4}.

Example 2 If A is the set of all dogs and B is the set of all cats
then A ∪ B is the set of animals which are either dogs or cats,
and A ∩ B = ϕ.

Example 3 If A is any set, then A ∪ A′ = $\mathcal{E}$ and A ∩ A′ = ϕ.

Example 4 With reference to Exercises 1.3, No. 2, which of the
following statements are correct?

(a) S = R ∩ V   (b) R = C ∩ P   (c) P = C ∩ T

The first two statements are correct, the third is not.

EXERCISES 1.5

1. Given that $A = \{3, 5, 7, 9, 11\}$, $B = \{3, 4, 5, 6, 7, 8\}$, $C = \{2, 4, 6, 8, 10\}$ and that the universal set is $\{2, 3, 4, 5, 6, 7, 8, 9, 10, 11\}$ find

(a) $A \cup B$ (b) $B \cap C$ (c) $A' \cap C$

(d) $A \cap (B \cup C)$ (e) $A' \cup (B' \cup C')$ (f) $(A' \cup B') \cup C'$

(g) $(B \cup C)'$ (h) $(A \cap B) \cup (A \cap C)$

2. Given that E is the set of all English speaking mathematicians, G the set of all German speaking mathematicians, R the set of all Russian speaking mathematicians, and $\mathscr{E}$ the set of all mathematicians, describe the following sets in words:

(a) $E \cup G$ (b) $R \cap G$ (c) $R \cap E'$

(d) $G' \cup E$ (e) $(E \cap R)'$ (f) $E \cup (G \cap R)$

(g) $(E' \cup R') \cap G$

3. Given that the universal set is the set of all positive integers, A is the set of all positive integers less than or equal to 6, E is the set of all even positive integers, and M is the set of all positive integers which are multiples of 3, find simple expressions in terms of A, E, and M for the following sets:

(a) $\{3, 6\}$

(b) $\{1, 3, 5\}$

(c) All positive integers which are multiples of 6.

(d) All even integers greater than 6.

(e) The set which contains all multiples of 3 and all odd integers.

4.* The set of all subsets of a given set A, is called the *power set* of A, and is written P(A). Show that the number of elements in P(A) is 2^n, where n is the number of elements in A. If $A = \{a, b, c\}$ and $B = \{b, c, d\}$ write out the elements of the sets P(A), P(B) and P(A ∩ B).

1.6 Venn-Euler Diagrams

A pictorial representation of sets is often useful in indicating and verifying relationships between sets. One such pictorial representation is called a *Venn-Euler* diagram.

In a Venn-Euler diagram the universal set is represented by the set of points inside some rectangle, and other sets within the universal set are represented by sets of points inside closed regions (circles, etc.) within this rectangle. By shading appropriate areas, all combinations of sets can be represented pictorially. We illustrate by example.

Example 1

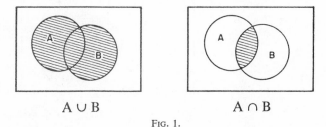

A ∪ B   A ∩ B

Fig. 1.

Example 2

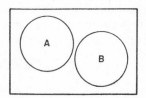

Disjoint Sets (i.e. A ∩ B = ϕ)

Fig. 2.

Example 3   Verify the relationship A ∪ (A ∩ B) = A

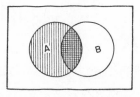

Fig. 3.

In the diagram the region A is shaded vertically and the region A ∩ B is shaded horizontally. A ∪ (A ∩ B) is the region containing either vertical or horizontal shading, or both. Hence A ∪ (A ∩ B) = A.

Example 4   Verify the relationship

$$A \cup (B \cap C) = (A \cup B) \cap (A \cup C)$$

In Fig. 4, B ∩ C is the region shaded vertically and A is the region shaded horizontally. Hence A ∪ (B ∩ C) is the region in Fig. 4 which contains either horizontal or vertical shading, or both.

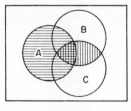

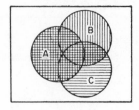

Fig. 4.   Fig. 5.

In Fig. 5, A ∪ B is the region shaded vertically and A ∪ C is the region shaded horizontally. Hence (A ∪ B) ∩ (A ∪ C) is the region which is shaded both horizontally and vertically.

Hence, since the regions corresponding to A ∪ (B ∩ C) and (A ∪ B) ∩ (A ∪ C) are identical, it follows that

$$A \cup (B \cap C) = (A \cup B) \cap (A \cup C).$$

EXERCISES 1.6

1. Assuming that A and B are not disjoint sets indicate the following sets on Venn-Euler diagrams:

(a) A′   (b) A′ ∩ B′   (c) (A ∪ B)′

(d) A′ ∩ B   (e) A ∪ B′   (f) A′ ∪ B′

(g) (A ∩ B)′

Deduce two set relationships from your diagrams.

2.* Assuming that A ∩ B ∩ C ≠ φ indicate the following sets on the same Venn-Euler diagram:

(a) A ∩ B ∩ C   (b) A ∩ B ∩ C′   (c) A ∩ B′ ∩ C

(d) A′ ∩ B ∩ C   (e) A ∩ B′ ∩ C′   (f) A′ ∩ B ∩ C′

(g) A′ ∩ B′ ∩ C   (h) A′ ∩ B′ ∩ C′

Hence simplify the set

$$(A \cap B \cap C) \cup (A \cap B \cap C') \cup (A \cap B' \cap C) \cup (A' \cap B \cap C)$$
$$\cup (A \cap B' \cap C') \cup (A' \cap B \cap C') \cup (A' \cap B' \cap C)$$
$$\cup (A' \cap B' \cap C').$$

[You may assume that $A \cap B \cap C = A \cap (B \cap C)$.]

3. Use Venn-Euler diagrams to verify that

(a) $A \cup (A' \cap B) = A \cup B$

(b) $A \cap (B \cup C) = (A \cap B) \cup (A \cap C)$

(c) $(A \cup B) \cap (A' \cup C) \cap (B \cup C) = (A \cup B) \cap (A' \cup C)$

1.7 Laws of Operation

To establish an identity in the algebra of sets we can either appeal to an appropriate Venn-Euler diagram or we can proceed thus.

Example 1* Show that $A \cup (A \cap B) = A$.

Our method of attack is based on the fact that if $X \subset Y$ and $Y \subset X$ then it follows that $X = Y$. The argument is in two parts.

I. Let $x \in A$.

Then $\qquad x \in A \cup (A \cap B)$.

Hence $\qquad A \subset A \cup (A \cap B) \qquad \qquad ....(1)$

II. Let $x \in A \cup (A \cap B)$.

Then $\qquad x \in A$ or $x \in A \cap B$

That is $\qquad x \in A$, or $x \in A$ and $x \in B$

$\therefore \qquad x \in A$.

Hence $\qquad A \cup (A \cap B) \subset A \qquad \qquad ....(2)$

Hence by results (1) and (2) it follows that

$$A \cup (A \cap B) = A$$

Example 2* Show that $(A \cup B)' = A' \cap B'$.
We proceed as in Example 1.

I. Let $x \in (A \cup B)'$

Then $\qquad\qquad x \notin A \cup B$

$\therefore \qquad\qquad\quad x \notin A$ and $x \notin B$

$\therefore \qquad\qquad\quad x \in A'$ and $x \in B'$

$\therefore \qquad\qquad\quad x \in A' \cap B'$

Hence $\qquad\quad (A \cup B)' \subset A' \cap B' \qquad\qquad ....(1)$

II. Similarly $\quad A' \cap B' \subset (A \cup B)' \qquad\qquad ....(2)$

It follows from results (1) and (2) that

$$(A \cup B)' = A' \cap B'.$$

We now list the basic laws which are valid in the algebra of sets. Some of these laws are intuitively obvious, others are less familiar. The validity of each law can be established as above.

Commutative Laws

(1a) $A \cup B = B \cup A$ $\qquad$ (1b) $A \cap B = B \cap A$

Associative Laws

(2a) $A \cup (B \cup C)$ $\qquad$ (2b) $A \cap (B \cap C)$
$\qquad = (A \cup B) \cup C$ $\qquad\qquad = (A \cap B) \cap C$

Distributive Laws

(3a) $A \cup (B \cap C)$ $\qquad$ (3b) $A \cap (B \cup C)$
$\qquad = (A \cup B) \cap (A \cup C)$ $\qquad\quad = (A \cap B) \cup (A \cap C)$

Idempotent Laws

(4a) $A \cup A = A$ $\qquad\qquad$ (4b) $A \cap A = A$

Laws of Absorption

(5a) $A \cup (A \cap B) = A$ $\qquad$ (5b) $A \cap (A \cup B) = A$

Laws of Complementation

(6a) $A \cup A' = \mathscr{E}$ $\qquad\qquad$ (6b) $A \cap A' = \phi$

Law of Double Complementation

(7) $(A')' = A$

Laws of De Morgan

(8a) $(A \cup B)' = A' \cap B'$ (8b) $(A \cap B)' = A' \cup B'$

Operations with ϕ and $\mathscr{E}$

(9a) $\mathscr{E} \cup A = \mathscr{E}$ (9b) $\phi \cap A = \phi$

(10a) $\phi \cup A = A$ (10b) $\mathscr{E} \cap A = A$

(11a) $\phi' = \mathscr{E}$ (11b) $\mathscr{E}' = \phi$

Laws of Set Inclusion

(12) If $A \subset B$ and $B \subset C$ then $A \subset C$.

(13) If $A \subset B$ and $A \subset C$ then $A \subset B \cap C$.

(14) If $A \subset B$ then $A \subset B \cup C$ where C is an arbitrary set.

(15) $A \subset B$ if and only if $B' \subset A'$.

Notes

I. The meanings of the words commutative, associative and distributive will be discussed further in Chapter 2.

II. The associative laws indicate that we may omit brackets in expressions of the form $A \cup B \cup C$, $A \cap B \cap C$, etc., without the introduction of any ambiguity.

III. Many of the above laws continue to hold in ordinary algebra if $\cup$ is replaced by $+$ and $\cap$ by $\times$ but some do not. For example, laws (1a), (1b), (2a), (2b) and (3b) continue to hold but law (3a) does not since $A + BC \neq (A + B)(A + C)$ in ordinary algebra.

IV. An examination of the above laws show that they occur in dual pairs, i.e., if, in any law in the algebra of sets, each union is replaced by intersection, each intersection by union, ϕ by $\mathscr{E}$ and $\mathscr{E}$ by ϕ, then the resulting expression is also a law in the algebra of sets. Each law is said to be the *dual* of the other. It follows that if we take any identity in the algebra of sets, which has been derived by means of the above laws, and replace each union by intersection, etc., then the resulting expression is also an identity. This is the *principle of duality*.

Example 3   Show that if $A \subset B$ and $A \subset C$ then $A \subset B \cap C$.

Let	$x \in A$
Then	$x \in B$ and $x \in C$
$\therefore$	$x \in B \cap C$
$\therefore$	$A \subset B \cap C.$

Example 4   Show that $A \subset B$ if and only if $B' \subset A'$.

I. Given $B' \subset A'$, let $x \in A$.

Then	$x \notin A'$
$\therefore$	$x \notin B'$ since $B' \subset A'$
$\therefore$	$x \in B$
$\therefore$	$A \subset B.$

II. Given $A \subset B$, let $x \in B'$.

Then	$x \notin B$
$\therefore$	$x \notin A$ since $A \subset B$
$\therefore$	$x \in A'$
$\therefore$	$B' \subset A'.$

Hence $A \subset B$ if and only if $B' \subset A'$.

EXERCISES 1.7

1. Show that $A \cup B = B \cup A$ and $A \cap B = B \cap A$.
2. Show that $A \cap (A \cup B) = A$.
3. Show that $A \cap (B \cup C) = (A \cap B) \cup (A \cap C)$.
4. Show that $(A \cap B)' = A' \cup B'$.
5. Show that (*a*) if $A \subset B$ and $B \subset C$ then $A \subset C$;
   (*b*) if $A \subset B$ then $A \subset B \cup C$ where C is an arbitrary set;
   (*c*)* $A \subset B$ if and only if $A \cap B' = \phi$.

1.8 The Simplification of Expressions Involving Sets

By using the laws of set theory, expressions involving sets may often be greatly simplified, just as expressions in ordinary algebra are simplified. We illustrate by example.

Example 1*   Show that $A \cup (A' \cap B) = A \cup B$

$$\begin{aligned}
A \cup (A' \cap B) &= (A \cup A') \cap (A \cup B) && \text{(Law 3a)} \\
&= \mathscr{E} \cap (A \cup B) && \text{(Law 6a)} \\
&= A \cup B && \text{(Law 10b)}
\end{aligned}$$

Example 2   Simplify $\{A \cap (A' \cup B)\} \cup \{B \cap (A' \cup B')\}$

$$\begin{aligned}
&\{A \cap (A' \cup B)\} \cup \{B \cap (A' \cup B')\} \\
&= \{(A \cap A') \cup (A \cap B)\} \cup \{(B \cap A') \cup (B \cap B')\} && \text{(Law 3b)} \\
&= \{\phi \cup (A \cap B)\} \cup \{(B \cap A') \cup \phi\} && \text{(Law 6b)} \\
&= (A \cap B) \cup \{(B \cap A') \cup \phi\} && \text{(Law 10a)} \\
&= (A \cap B) \cup \{\phi \cup (B \cap A')\} && \text{(Law 1a)} \\
&= (A \cap B) \cup (B \cap A') && \text{(Law 10a)} \\
&= (B \cap A) \cup (B \cap A') && \text{(Law 1b)} \\
&= B \cap (A \cup A') && \text{(Law 3b)} \\
&= B \cap \mathscr{E} && \text{(Law 6a)} \\
&= \mathscr{E} \cap B && \text{(Law 1b)} \\
&= B && \text{(Law 10b)}
\end{aligned}$$

Example 3*   Show that $(A \cup B \cup C)' = A' \cap B' \cap C'$ and $(A \cap B \cap C)' = A' \cup B' \cup C'$. Generalise these results.

$$\begin{aligned}
(A \cup B \cup C)' &= \{A \cup (B \cup C)\}' \\
&= A' \cap (B \cup C)' && \text{by De Morgan's law 1} \\
&= A' \cap (B' \cap C') && \text{by De Morgan's law 1} \\
&= A' \cap B' \cap C'
\end{aligned}$$

Taking the dual of this result, we immediately obtain $(A \cap B \cap C)' = A' \cup B' \cup C'$. The results obviously generalise to

$$(A_1 \cup A_2 \cup A_3 \cup \ldots \cup A_n)' = A_1' \cap A_2' \cap A_3' \cap \ldots \cap A_n'$$

and

$$(A_1 \cap A_2 \cap A_3 \cap \ldots \cap A_n)' = A_1' \cup A_2' \cup A_3' \cup \ldots \cup A_n'$$

Example 4   Simplify

$$(A \cap B) \cup (A \cap B') \cup (A' \cap B) \cup (A' \cap B').$$

$$(A \cap B) \cup (A \cap B') \cup (A' \cap B) \cup (A' \cap B')$$
$$= \{A \cap (B \cup B')\} \cup \{A' \cap (B \cup B')\}$$
$$= (A \cap \mathscr{E}) \cup (A' \cap \mathscr{E})$$
$$= A \cup A'$$
$$= \mathscr{E}$$

Example 5 Simplify $A' \cup B' \cup C' \cup (A \cap B \cap C)$.

$$A' \cup B' \cup C' \cup (A \cap B \cap C) = (A \cap B \cap C)' \cup (A \cap B \cap C)$$
$$= \mathscr{E}$$

Example 6 Simplify $(A \cap B) \cup (A' \cap C) \cup (B \cap C)$.

$$(A \cap B) \cup (A' \cap C) \cup (B \cap C)$$
$$= (A \cap B) \cup (A' \cap C) \cup \{(A \cap B \cap C) \cup (A' \cap B \cap C)\}$$
$$= \{(A \cap B) \cup (A \cap B \cap C)\} \cup \{(A' \cap C) \cup (A' \cap B \cap C)\}$$
$$= (A \cap B) \cup (A' \cap C)$$

Example 7 Show that $(A \cap B \cap C) \cup (A' \cap C) \cup (B' \cap C) = C$.

$$(A \cap B \cap C) \cup (A' \cap C) \cup (B' \cap C)$$
$$= \{(A \cap B) \cup A' \cup B'\} \cap C$$
$$= \{(A \cap B) \cup (A \cap B)'\} \cap C$$
$$= \mathscr{E} \cap C$$
$$= C$$

EXERCISES 1.8

1. Simplify

(*a*) $(A \cap B) \cup (A \cap B \cap C')$

(*b*) $A \cup B' \cup (A' \cap B)$

(*c*) $\{(A \cup B' \cup C) \cap (A' \cap B)\} \cup (A \cap B \cap C)$

(*d*) $(A \cap B' \cap C') \cup (A \cap B' \cap C' \cap D) \cup (A \cap C')$

(*e*) $(A \cap B) \cup (A \cap B' \cap C)$

(*f*) $(A \cap B \cap C) \cup (A \cap B' \cap C) \cup (A \cap C')$

2. Simplify

(a) $(X \cup Y) \cap (X \cup Y')$

(b) $(X \cup Y \cup Z') \cap (X' \cap Y' \cap Z)$

(c) $\{X \cup (X \cap Y')\} \cap \{X \cup (Y \cap Z)\}$

(d) $(X' \cup Y) \cap \{X \cup Y \cup (X \cap Y)\}$

(e) $\{(X \cup Y) \cap (X' \cup Y')\} \cup (X \cap Y)$

(f) $\{(X \cup Y) \cap (Y \cup Z) \cap (X' \cup Z')\} \cup (X \cap Y \cap Z') \cup (Y \cap Z)$

3. Simplify

(a) $(A \cup B)' \cup (A' \cup B)'$

(b) $(A' \cap B')' \cup (A \cup B)'$

(c) $\{(A \cap B) \cup (A' \cap B')\}'$

(d) $\{(A \cap B) \cup (A \cap B') \cup (A' \cap B')\}'$

(e) $(A \cup B \cup C)' \cup (A' \cap B)'$

(f) $\{(A \cap C) \cup (B \cap D)\}' \cup \{(A' \cap B) \cup (C' \cap D)\}'$

4. What is the dual of the identity

$$(A \cap B) \cup (A' \cap C) \cup (B \cap C) = (A \cap B) \cup (A' \cap C)?$$

5. Simplify $(A \cap B) \cup (A' \cap C \cap D' \cap E) \cup (B' \cap C \cap D')$.
What is the dual of this result?

1.9 Applications of Set Theory to Arithmetic and Logical Problems

Certain arithmetic problems can often be quickly solved by the use of a Venn-Euler diagram. We illustrate by example.

Example 1 An investigation of the sporting interests of 100 students yielded the following data: 50 played badminton, 43 played squash, 45 played tennis, 12 played badminton and squash, 13 played squash and tennis, 15 played tennis and badminton, and 5 played all three sports. Is the data consistent?

Let B denote the set of badminton playing students,
   S denote the set of squash playing students,
   T denote the set of tennis playing students.

An appropriate Venn-Euler diagram is therefore—

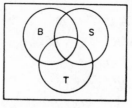

FIG. 6.

We will use the notation $n(A)$ to denote the number of elements in the set A. We therefore know that

$$n(B) = 50, \qquad n(S) = 43, \qquad n(T) = 45,$$
$$n(B \cap S) = 12, \qquad n(S \cap T) = 13, \qquad n(T \cap B) = 15,$$
$$n(B \cap S \cap T) = 5.$$

The number of elements in the region common to all three circles is therefore 5 and this can be indicated on the Venn-Euler diagram. Also since

$$n(B \cap S \cap T') = n(B \cap S) - n(B \cap S \cap T)$$

we have that $n(B \cap S \cap T') = 12 - 5 = 7$.

Similarly $\qquad n(S \cap T \cap B') = 13 - 5 = 8,$

and $n(T \cap B \cap S') = 15 - 5 = 10$. These figures can also be attached to the corresponding regions in the Venn-Euler diagram which now looks like

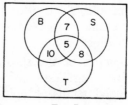

FIG. 7.

Hence $\qquad n(B \cap S' \cap T') = n(B) - 7 - 5 - 10$
$$= 50 - 22$$
$$= 28$$

$$n(S \cap T' \cap B') = n(S) - 7 - 5 - 8$$
$$= 43 - 20$$
$$= 23$$
$$n(T \cap B' \cap S') = 50 - 10 - 5 - 8$$
$$= 45 - 23$$
$$= 22$$

and these figures can also be attached to the corresponding regions on the Venn-Euler diagram. We finally obtain

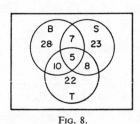

FIG. 8.

Hence the total number of students

$$= 28 + 7 + 5 + 10 + 23 + 8 + 22$$
$$= 103$$

Hence the data is inconsistent.

Example 2 In a battle involving 100 men, 42 were shot in the head, 43 in the arm, 32 in the leg, 5 in the head and arm, 8 in the arm and leg, 6 in the leg and head. How many were shot in all three places?

Let H be the set of men shot in the head,
  A be the set of men shot in the arm,
  L be the set of men shot in the leg.

Then we know that

$$n(H) = 42, \qquad n(A) = 43, \qquad n(L) = 32,$$
$$n(H \cap A) = 5, \qquad n(A \cap L) = 8, \qquad n(L \cap H) = 6.$$

Let $n(H \cap A \cap L) = x$.

Then, as indicated in the previous example, a Venn-Euler diagram can be drawn, and numbers attached to the various regions thus

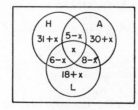

FIG. 9.

Hence $42 + 38 + 18 + x = 100$

∴ $x = 2$

∴   2 men were shot in all three places.

The laws of set inclusion and the methods of simplification in the algebra of sets can be used to solve certain logical problems. We illustrate by example.

Example 3   What conclusion can be drawn from the following statements?

    (*a*) Good losers are always popular.
    (*b*) Happy men are never lonely.
    (*c*) Bad losers do not enjoy playing tennis.
    (*d*) Unhappy men are unpopular.

Let the universal set be the set of all men, and denote other sets as follows—

    G is the set of men who are good losers,
    P is the set of men who are always popular,
    H is the set of happy men,
    L is the set of lonely men,
    T is the set of men who enjoy playing tennis.

Then the above statements are given symbolically by

    (*a*) $G \subset P$
    (*b*) $H \subset L'$
    (*c*) $G' \subset T'$
    (*d*) $H' \subset P'$

From (*c*) $T \subset G$ (Law 15)

From (a) $G \subset P$
From (d) $P \subset H$　　　(Law 15)
From (b) $H \subset L'$
$\therefore$ $T \subset G \subset P \subset H \subset L'$
Hence $T \subset L'$
Hence men who enjoy playing tennis are never lonely.

Example 4 Members of a certain club had to adhere to the following regulations—

(a) On any occasion when a tie is not worn, a scarf must be worn.

(b) On any occasion when a tie and a scarf are both worn, a hat must not be worn.

(c) On any occasion when a hat is worn, or a tie is not worn, a scarf must not be worn.

Help the club members by simplifying the rules.
Let T be the set of occasions on which a tie must be worn,
　　S be the set of occasions on which a scarf must be worn,
　　H be the set of occasions on which a hat must be worn.

Then (a) $T' \subset S$
　　(b) $T \cap S \subset H'$
　　(c) $H \cup T' \subset S'$

Now using Exercises 1.7, No. 5(c), we immediately have that

(a) $T' \cap S'$　　　$= \phi$
(b) $(T \cap S) \cap H = \phi$
(c) $(H \cup T') \cap S = \phi$

Hence $(T' \cap S') \cup (T \cap S \cap H) \cup \{(H \cup T') \cap S\} = \phi$

$\therefore$ $(T' \cap S') \cup (T \cap S \cap H) \cup (H \cap S) \cup (S \cap T') = \phi$

$\therefore$ $T' \cup (T \cap S \cap H) \cup (H \cap S) = \phi$

$\therefore$ $T' \cup (H \cap S) = \phi$

$\therefore$ $T' = \phi$ and $H \cap S = \phi$

$\therefore$ $T = \mathscr{E}$ and $(H \cap S)' = \mathscr{E}$

Hence wear a tie on all occasions and never wear both a hat and scarf together.

EXERCISES 1.9

1. In a group of 100 students, 48 drank coffee, 48 drank lemonade, 36 drank tea, 15 drank both coffee and lemonade, 12 drank both lemonade and tea, 10 drank both tea and coffee, and 7 drank coffee, lemonade and tea. Is the data consistent?

2. The qualifications of 100 teachers were investigated and the following data obtained: 68 were qualified to teach English, 15 to teach Mathematics, 51 to teach Science, 13 to teach English and Mathematics, 12 to teach Mathematics and Science, 17 to teach Science and English, and 8 to teach all three subjects. Is the data consistent?

3. To investigate the popularity of three soap powders X, Y, Z, 100 housewives were asked to complete a questionnaire and the following information was obtained: 42 housewives had used brand X, 50 had used brand Y, 48 had used brand Z, 12 had used brand X and brand Y, 18 had used brand Y and brand Z, and 13 had used brand Z and brand X. How many housewives had used all three brands?

4. What can be deduced from the following statements?
   (a) Abstract thinkers are not practical men.
   (b) Mathematicians enjoy using symbols.
   (c) Men who do not believe in immortality are practical.
   (d) Men who do not enjoy abstract thinking do not enjoy using symbols.

5. What can be deduced from the following premises?
   (a) There is no box of mine here that I dare open.
   (b) My writing desk is made of rosewood.
   (c) All my boxes are painted, except what are here.
   (d) All my rosewood boxes are unpainted.
   (e) There is no box of mine that I dare not open, unless it is full of live scorpions. (From Lewis Carroll.)
   (Assume that a writing desk is a type of box.)

6. To qualify for reduced subscription rates to a certain magazine a person must satisfy the following regulations:
   (a) If the person is married then he must be over 21 and employed.
   (b) If the person is unemployed he must be under 21 and single.
   (c) Each person must be either under 21 or unemployed.

   Simplify these regulations.

Chapter Two

BINARY OPERATIONS

2.1

When two real numbers are added together the result is another real number. This is also the case when one real number is subtracted from another. Addition and subtraction are thus rules of combination, which, when applied to elements of the set of real numbers, yield results which also belong to this set. Similarly the operation of union, when applied to subsets of some universal set, yields a result which is also a subset of this universal set.

The operations $+$, $-$, and $\cup$, as described above are all examples of *binary operations*, which are precisely defined as follows:

Definition: Given a set of elements M, then a binary operation $*$ on the set M is a rule of combination which assigns to each *ordered pair* of elements $a, b \in$ M a unique element $c \in$ M. We write symbolically that $c = a * b$.

Example 1 Let A be the set of all positive integers. Then the operation of addition on the set A is a binary operation, for if $a, b \in$ A then so is c where $c = a + b$.

Example 2 Let X be the set of all odd positive integers. Then the operation of addition on the set X is not a binary operation for if $a, b \in$ X then $c \notin$ X where $c = a + b$.

Example 3 Let M be the set of all integers. Then the operation of division on the set M is not a binary operation for $c = a \div b$ is not always an element of M, when $a, b \in$ M. For example, when $a = 2$, $b = 3$ then $c = 0.6666 \ldots$ which is not an element of M.

21

EXERCISES 2.1

1. Which of the following are binary operations on the sets indicated?

(a) multiplication on the set of all positive integers,
(b) subtraction on the set of all positive integers,
(c) subtraction on the set of all integers,
(d) multiplication on the set of all complex numbers,
(e) multiplication on the set of all even positive integers,
(f) subtraction on the set of all rational numbers,
(g) intersection on the set of all subsets of some universal set.

2.2 Commutative, Associative, Distributive, and Idempotent Binary Operations

Defn.: A binary operation $*$ on a set of elements M is said to be *commutative*, if and only if, for every $a, b \in M$,

$$a * b = b * a$$

Defn.: A binary operation $*$ on a set of elements M is said to be *associative* if and only if, for every $a, b, c \in M$,

$$a * (b * c) = (a * b) * c$$

Defn.: The binary operation $*$ on a set of elements M is said to be *distributive over* the binary operation $\circ$ on the same set of elements, if and only if, for every $a, b, c \in M$,

$$a * (b \circ c) = (a * b) \circ (a * c)$$

Defn.: The binary operation $*$ is said to be *idempotent* on a set of elements M, if and only if, for every $a \in M$,

$$a * a = a$$

Defn.: An element e in a set M is said to be a unit element with respect to the binary operation $*$ on M if and only if, for every $a \in M$,

$$a * e = e * a = a$$

Example 1 Discuss the binary operations of addition and multiplication on the set of all real numbers.

Addition is commutative since $a + b = b + a$ and associative since $a + (b + c) = (a + b) + c$. It is not distributive over multiplication since $a + bc \neq (a + b) . (a + c)$ and not idempotent since $a + a \neq a$.

Multiplication is commutative and associative, since $a \cdot b = b \cdot a$ and $a \cdot (b \cdot c) = (a \cdot b) \cdot c$. It is also distributive over addition since $a \cdot (b + c) = a \cdot b + a \cdot c$, but it is not idempotent since $a \cdot a \neq a$.

0 is an identity element for addition since $a + 0 = 0 + a = a$ and 1 is an identity element for multiplication since $a \cdot 1 = 1 \cdot a = a$.

Example 2 In the algebra of sets the operations $\cup$, $\cap$ are both commutative, associative, idempotent, and each one distributes over the other. The null set ϕ is the unit element for the operation $\cup$, and the universal set $\mathscr{E}$ is the unit element for the operation $\cap$.

Example 3 The binary operations $\sim$ and $\circ$ on the set of all real numbers are defined by

$$a \sim b = |a - b|, \qquad a \circ b = a.$$

Show that $\sim$ is commutative but not associative, $\circ$ is associative but not commutative, and that $\sim$ distributes over $\circ$.

I. Since
$$\begin{aligned} a \sim b &= |a - b| \\ &= |b - a| \\ &= b \sim a \end{aligned}$$

$\therefore \sim$ is commutative.

That $\sim$ is not associative can be seen readily by giving a, b, c specific values. If $a = 1$, $b = 2$, $c = 5$, then

$$a \sim (b \sim c) = 2 \text{ and } (a \sim b) \sim c = 4.$$

Hence $\sim$ is not associative.

II. Since $a \circ b = a$ and $b \circ a = b$ it follows that $\circ$ is not commutative.

However $\qquad a \circ (b \circ c) = a \circ b = a$

and $\qquad (a \circ b) \circ c = a \circ c = a$

$\therefore \qquad a \circ (b \circ c) = (a \circ b) \circ c$

Hence $\circ$ is associative.

III. Since $\qquad a \sim (b \circ c) = a \sim b$

and $\qquad (a \sim b) \circ (a \sim c) = a \sim b$

$\therefore \qquad a \sim (b \circ c) = (a \sim b) \circ (a \sim c)$

Hence $\sim$ distributes over $\circ$.

EXERCISES 2.2

1. Show that the binary operation of subtraction on the set of all real numbers is not commutative and not associative.

2. Given that $a * b = a$, show that the binary operation $*$ on the set of all real numbers is idempotent.

3. Given that $a * b = \max (a, b)$ and $a \circ b = \min (a, b)$, show that the binary operations $*$ and $\circ$ on the set of real numbers are both commutative, associative and idempotent.

4. Given that $a * b = \frac{1}{2}(a + b)$ show that the binary operation $*$ on the set of all real numbers is commutative but not associative.

5. The binary operation $\oplus$ on the set of all real numbers is defined by $a \oplus b = a + b + ab$. Show that $\oplus$ is both commutative and associative. Is there a unit element corresponding to $\oplus$?

6. The binary operation $+$ in the algebra of sets is defined by $A + B = (A \cap B') \cup (A' \cap B)$. Show that $\cap$ distributes over $+$.

7. The binary operation $\times$ in the algebra of sets is defined by $A \times B = (A \cap B) \cup (A' \cap B')$. Show that $\cup$ distributes over $\times$.

Chapter Three

THE ALGEBRA OF PROPOSITIONS

3.1 *Introduction*

The word *proposition* is used with many shades of meaning in everyday life. To us it will mean a statement which is either *true* or *false*, but not both. Note that no attempt will be made to give precise definitions for the terms proposition, true and false. For our purposes it is sufficient to assume the existence of a large class of statements which are such that we can assign to each one either the *truth value* T or the truth value F. (T and F are, of course, convenient abbreviations for 'true' and 'false'.)

Example 1 The following statements are propositions:

(*a*) Today is Tuesday.
(*b*) The Moon is made of green cheese.
(*c*) $5 < 7$.
(*d*) All mathematicians are lazy.
(*e*) If it rains I shall get wet.
(*f*) Some men are stupid and pigs can fly.

Example 2 The following are not propositions:

(*a*) Oh, what a beautiful morning.
(*b*) Two lovely black eyes.
(*c*) Give me the book.
(*d*) When I consider how my light is spent.
(*e*) The statement you are reading is false.

It will be convenient to use $a, b, c, d, \ldots$ to denote propositions. Later these letters will be used without specific propositions in mind and it will then be convenient to refer to them as *propositional variables*.

25

3.2 *The Negation of a Proposition*

Let p be any proposition. Then we write the *negation of p* as p' (in some books $\neg\, p$) and define it to be the proposition 'it is false that p.'

Example 1 Let p be the proposition 'the door is locked'. Then p', the negation of p, is the proposition 'it is false that the door is locked', or, in better English, 'the door is not locked'.

Example 2 Let q be the proposition 'all men are honest'. Then q' is the proposition 'it is false that all men are honest'. This could be better phrased as 'not all men are honest'. A slightly dubious rephrasing would be 'all men are not honest' and a completely wrong attempt would be 'all men are dishonest' which is *not* the negation of q as defined above.

It is worth emphasising that the propositions p and p' must have *opposite* truth values, i.e. if p is a true proposition then p' is a false proposition and *vice versa*. Example 2 above illustrates this well. We can also tabulate the connection between p and p' as a *truth table* thus:

p	p'
T	F
F	T

The truth table here is simple and self-explanatory. Later we shall construct much more sophisticated truth tables representing propositions which are 'functions' of simpler propositions.

EXERCISES 3.2

1. Which of the following are propositions?
   (*a*) Confucius was a wise man.
   (*b*) Do not stand on the flowers.
   (*c*) There is no greatest prime number.
   (*d*) $6 > 341$.
   (*e*) As white as a sheet.
   (*f*) It will rain somewhere in London on July 23rd, 1992.
   (*g*) Is that a reasonable argument?
   (*h*) If $2 + 2 = 5$ then ice-cream is yellow.

2. Write, in reasonable English, the negations of the following propositions:

   (a) All students are industrious.
   (b) One side of Mercury always faces the Sun.
   (c) I like eating plums and I like drinking lemonade.
   (d) A power of 2 never ends in a 7.
   (e) Either the sun will be shining or I shall carry my umbrella.

3.3 Combinations of Propositions

Given two propositions p, q it is possible to form a new proposition by joining them with the *connective* 'or'. Thus, for example, from the propositions 'grass is green' and 'politicians never tell the truth' we could form the proposition 'grass is green or politicians never tell the truth'. Unfortunately in English the word 'or' is used both in an *inclusive* manner and in an *exclusive* manner. For example, in the proposition 'either this is a sparrow or this is a bird' it is possible for both statements to be the case and the 'or' is therefore used in an inclusive sense, whereas in the statement 'either I shall go to the pictures or I shall stay at home' it is not possible for both statements to be valid and the 'or' is therefore used in an exclusive sense.

To avoid ambiguity we must settle upon one of the two possibilities and in basic logic it is customary to interpret the use of the word 'or' in the inclusive sense. We are thus led to the following definition—given two propositions p, q we define the *disjunction* of p and q to be the proposition

either p or q or both

and we write it $p \lor q$. Quite often the words 'either' and 'or both' are omitted and we say that $p \lor q$ is the proposition 'p or q' remembering that the 'or' is to be interpreted in the inclusive sense. The proposition $p \lor q$ is completely specified by its truth table which we take to be:

p	q	$p \lor q$
T	T	T
T	F	T
F	T	T
F	F	F

Thus the proposition $p \lor q$ is false if and only if the propositions p, q are both false.

In a similar manner we can obtain a new proposition from two given propositions p, q by using the connective 'and'. We are thus led to defining the *conjunction* of p and q to be the proposition

$$\text{both } p \text{ and } q$$

and we write it $p \land q$. Quite often the word 'both' is omitted. The truth table for $p \land q$ is specified to be

p	q	$p \land q$
T	T	T
T	F	F
F	T	F
F	F	F

Thus the proposition $p \land q$ is true if and only if the propositions p, q are both true.

Example 1 Let p be the proposition 'Mathematicians are lazy' and q be the proposition 'Tennis racquets are expensive'.

Then

(a) $p \lor q$ is the proposition 'Mathematicians are lazy or tennis racquets are expensive'.

(b) $p' \land q$ is the proposition 'Some mathematicians are not lazy and tennis racquets are expensive'.

(c) $p' \lor q'$ is the proposition 'Either some mathematicians are not lazy or some tennis racquets are inexpensive'.

3.4 *Equality of Propositions*

We must first define what we mean by the *equality* of two propositions. We illustrate first by a simple example.

Example 1 Consider the propositions $(p \land q)'$ and $p' \lor q'$. Their truth tables are:

p	q	$(p \wedge q)'$
T	T	F
T	F	T
F	T	T
F	F	T

p	q	$p' \vee q'$
T	T	F
T	F	T
F	T	T
F	F	T

Note that the propositions $(p \wedge q)'$ and $p' \vee q'$ have *identical* truth values for all possible ways of assigning truth values to the component propositions p, q. It therefore seems natural to say that the propositions $(p \wedge q)'$ and $p' \vee q'$ are *equal*, and to write

$$(p \wedge q)' = p' \vee q'$$

The general definition of equality of propositions now suggests itself. Let two propositions l, m be functions of the propositional variables $p, q, r \dots$. Then we shall say that the propositions l, m are equal if they have identical truth values for all possible ways of assigning truth values to the propositional variables $p, q, r, \dots$.

Example 2 Show that $p \vee (q \wedge r) = (p \vee q) \wedge (p \vee r)$. Since each of the propositions $p \vee (q \wedge r)$ and $(p \vee q) \wedge (p \vee r)$ is a function of the three propositional variables p, q, r we must draw up truth tables for the two propositions, in which all possible ways of assigning truth-values to p, q, r are covered.

The truth-tables for $p \vee (q \wedge r)$ and $(p \vee q) \wedge (p \vee r)$ are as follows, their method of construction being self-explanatory:

p	q	r	$q \wedge r$	$p \vee (q \wedge r)$
T	T	T	T	T
T	T	F	F	T
T	F	T	F	T
T	F	F	F	T
F	T	T	T	T
F	T	F	F	F
F	F	T	F	F
F	F	F	F	F

p	q	r	$p \vee q$	$p \vee r$	$(p \vee q) \wedge (p \vee r)$
T	T	T	T	T	T
T	T	F	T	T	T
T	F	T	T	T	T
T	F	F	T	T	T
F	T	T	T	T	T
F	T	F	T	F	F
F	F	T	F	T	F
F	F	F	F	F	F

By comparison of the last columns in each table it follows that $p \vee (q \wedge r) = (p \vee q) \wedge (p \vee r)$.

Before investigating further the algebra of propositions it will be convenient to extend our use of the letters T and F. We will use T to represent any proposition which is always true and F to represent any proposition which is always false.

Example 3 It follows from the above that $p \vee p' = T$ and $p \wedge p' = F$ as can readily be appreciated by examination of their truth tables:

p	p'	$p \vee p'$
T	F	T
F	T	T

p	p'	$p \wedge p'$
T	F	F
F	T	F

Example 4 Show that $\{(p \vee q) \wedge (p \vee q')\} \vee p' = T$.
We construct a truth table for the proposition
$$(p \vee q) \wedge (p \vee q') \vee p':$$

p	q	$p \vee q$	$p \vee q'$	$(p \vee q) \wedge (p \vee q')$	$\{(p \vee q) \wedge (p \vee q')\} \vee p'$
T	T	T	T	T	T
T	F	T	T	T	T
F	T	T	F	F	T
F	F	F	T	F	T

It follows by examination of the final column of the truth table that $\{(p \vee q) \wedge (p \vee q')\} \vee p' = T$.

N.B. A proposition, such as the above, which is always true, no matter what truth values are assigned to its component propositions, is called a *tautology*.

EXERCISES 3.4

1. Let p be the proposition 'high-speed driving is dangerous' and q the proposition 'Confucius was a wise man'. Write down, in reasonable English the meanings of the following propositions:

(a) $p \land q$ (b) $p' \lor q$

(c) $(p \lor q)'$ (d) $(p \land q) \lor (p' \land q')$

(e) $(p \lor q) \land (p \land q)'$

2. Use the truth table technique to establish the following results, given that p, q, r are arbitrary propositions:

(a) $p \land q = q \land p$

(b) $p \lor (q \lor r) = (p \lor q) \lor r$

(c) $p \land (q \lor r) = (p \land q) \lor (p \land r)$

(d) $p \lor p = p$

(e) $p \lor (p \land q) = p$

(f) $(p')' = p$

(g) $(p \lor q)' = p' \land q'$

(h) $T \lor p = T$

(i) $F \land p = F$

(j) $F' = T$

3. Use the truth table technique to establish that the following propositional functions are tautologies:

(a) $(p \land q) \lor (p \land q') \lor (p' \land q) \lor (p' \land q')$

(b) $\{(p \lor q') \land (p' \lor q')\} \lor q$

(c) $\{p \land (p' \lor q)\}' \lor q$

3.5 The Algebra of Propositions

Given arbitrary propositions p, q, r the following propositional identities are easily established by the truth table technique:

Commutative Laws

(1a) $p \lor q = q \lor p$ (1b) $p \land q = q \land p$

Associative Laws

(2a) $p \lor (q \lor r)$ (2b) $p \land (q \land r)$
$= (p \lor q) \lor r$ $= (p \land q) \land r$

Distributive Laws

(3a) $p \lor (q \land r)$ (3b) $p \land (q \lor r)$
$= (p \lor q) \land (p \lor r)$ $= (p \land q) \lor (p \land r)$

Idempotent Laws

(4a) $p \lor p = p$ (4b) $p \land p = p$

Laws of Absorption

(5a) $p \lor (p \land q) = p$ (5b) $p \land (p \lor q) = p$

Laws of Complementation

(6a) $p \lor p' = T$ (6b) $p \land p' = F$

Laws of Double Complementation

(7) $(p')' = p$

Laws of De Morgan

(8a) $(p \lor q)' = p' \land q'$ (8b) $(p \land q)' = p' \lor q'$

Operations with F and T

(9a) $T \lor p = T$ (9b) $F \land p = F$
(10a) $F \lor p = p$ (10b) $T \land p = p$
(11a) $F' = T$ (11b) $T' = F$

A comparison of the above laws with the laws of set theory (pages 10 and 11) reveals a remarkable similarity. Indeed the algebra of propositions is identical with the algebra of sets apart from the changes of symbolism indicated in the following table:

Algebra of Sets	Algebra of Propositions
A, B, C	p, q, r
$\cup$	$\lor$
$\cap$	$\land$
$\mathscr{E}$	T
ϕ	F

Notes

1. It follows that the methods of simplification outlined in Chapter 1 can be used in the algebra of propositions.

2. The algebra of sets and the algebra of propositions are both examples of *Boolean algebras*. The interested reader is referred to J. E. Whitesitt's excellent book *Boolean Algebra and its Applications* (Addison-Wesley, 1961) for further information.

Example 1 Simplify the propositional expression
$$\{p \wedge (p' \vee q)\} \vee \{q \wedge (p \wedge q)'\}.$$

$$
\begin{aligned}
\{p \wedge (p' \vee q)\} &\vee \{q \wedge (p \wedge q)'\} \\
&= \{p \wedge (p' \vee q)\} \vee \{q \wedge (p' \vee q')\} \\
&= (p \wedge p') \vee (p \wedge q) \vee (q \wedge p') \vee (q \wedge q') \\
&= F \vee (p \wedge q) \vee (q \wedge p') \vee F \\
&= (p \wedge q) \vee (q \wedge p') \\
&= q \wedge (p \vee p') \\
&= q \wedge T \\
&= q
\end{aligned}
$$

Example 2 Show that the proposition
$$\{(p \vee q') \wedge (p' \vee q')\} \vee q$$
is a tautology. (Cf. Exercises 3.4, No. 3*b*.)

$$
\begin{aligned}
\{(p \vee q') \wedge (p' \vee q')\} &\vee q \\
&= \{(p \wedge p') \vee (p \wedge q') \vee (q' \wedge p') \vee (q' \wedge q')\} \vee q \\
&= \{F \vee (p \wedge q') \vee (q' \wedge p') \vee q'\} \vee q \\
&= (p \wedge q') \vee (q' \wedge p') \vee T \\
&= T
\end{aligned}
$$

Hence $\{(p \vee q') \wedge (p' \vee q')\} \vee q$ is a tautology.

EXERCISES 3.5

1. Simplify

    (a) $(p' \wedge q') \vee (p' \wedge q' \wedge r')$

    (b) $p' \wedge \{q' \wedge (p' \vee q)\}$

    (c) $\{(p' \vee q' \vee r) \wedge (p \wedge r)\} \vee \{p \wedge (q' \vee r)\}$

(d) $(p' \wedge q') \vee (p' \wedge q \wedge r) \vee (p \vee q')'$

(e) $\{(p \vee q) \wedge (p' \vee r) \wedge (q' \vee r')\} \vee \{(p \vee q) \wedge r'\}'$

(f) $(p \wedge q) \vee (p \wedge r) \vee (q' \wedge r)$

(g) $\{(p \wedge r) \vee (q \vee s)\}' \vee \{(p' \wedge q) \vee (r' \wedge s)\}'$

2. Show that the following propositions are tautologies:

(a) $(p \wedge q) \vee (p \wedge q') \vee (p' \wedge q) \vee (p' \wedge q')$

(b) $\{(p \vee q') \wedge (p' \vee q')\} \vee q$

(c) $\{p \wedge (p' \vee q)\} \vee (p' \wedge q) \vee q'$

(d) $\{(p' \vee q) \wedge (r' \vee q')\}' \wedge (p' \vee r') \vee (p \wedge q' \wedge r')'$

(e) $\{(p \wedge q)' \wedge (q' \vee s')\}' \vee (p' \vee q')$

3.6 Further Combinations of Propositions

Given two propositions p, q we write the *conditional* or *implication* of p, q as $p \rightarrow q$ and define it to be the proposition

if p then q

The proposition $p \rightarrow q$ is completely specified by its truth table which we *define* to be

p	q	$p \rightarrow q$
T	T	T
T	F	F
F	T	T
F	F	T

The first two lines of the truth table for the proposition $p \rightarrow q$ are usually acceptable to most students of mathematics. The same cannot be said for the last two lines which are often the cause of comment. The decision to assign the truth value T to the proposition $p \rightarrow q$ when p is a false proposition, irrespective of the truth value of the proposition q, is to some extent an arbitrary one, but it is a *reasonable* decision. The confusion is caused by the fact that, in everyday life, when a statement of the form 'if p then q' is used the proposition p is usually true and the propositions p, q are normally related. Symbolic logic however must cater for situations where either or both of these restrictions do not apply.

Example 1 The proposition 'if bananas are purple then $2 + 2 = 4$' is a true proposition.

Example 2 The proposition 'if men have wings then cigarettes are coming down in price' is also a true proposition.

Example 3* Show that $p \to q = p' \vee q$.

That this is the case is obvious by examination of the truthtables for $p \to q$ and $p' \vee q$:

p	q	p'	$p \to q$	$p' \wedge q$
T	T	F	T	T
T	F	F	F	F
F	T	T	T	T
F	F	T	T	T

$$\therefore \ p \to q = p' \vee q$$

It should be noted that, quite often in mathematical literature the proposition $p \to q$ is not worded 'if p then q' but in some alternative fashion. We tabulate some of the possibilities for future reference:

if p then q
p is sufficient for q
q is necessary for p
p only if q
q if p
p implies q
q follows from p

N.B. It should be emphasised that the fourth expression in the above table for the proposition $p \to q$ requires careful handling. This is because the statements 'p if q' and 'p only if q' are often mis-used in everyday speech. For example, a person may declare 'I shall go out if it remains fair' whereas in actual fact he means 'I shall go out only if it remains fair'. The first version does not preclude the possibility of him going out even if it is raining and it is unlikely that that is what he intended.

Example 4   Express in different ways the statement 'if $f(x)$ has a relative maximum at $x = a$ then $f'(a) = 0$'.

Alternative versions of this statement are:

(a) That $f(x)$ has a relative maximum at $x = a$ is sufficient for $f'(a) = 0$.

(b) $f'(a) = 0$ is necessary for $f(x)$ to have a relative maximum at $x = a$.

(c) $f(x)$ has a relative maximum at $x = a$ only if $f'(a) = 0$.

(d) $f'(a) = 0$ if $f(x)$ has a relative maximum at $x = a$.

(e) That $f(x)$ has a relative maximum at $x = a$ implies that $f'(a) = 0$.

(f) $f'(a) = 0$ follows from the fact that $f(x)$ has a relative maximum at $x = a$.

Note the slight changes in wording to improve the readability of some of the statements.

The final combination of two given propositions p, q which we shall examine is known as the *biconditional* or *equivalence* of p, q. We write this proposition as $p \leftrightarrow q$ and define it to be the proposition

$$p \text{ if and only if } q$$

It is completely specified by its truth table:

p	q	$p \leftrightarrow q$
T	T	T
T	F	F
F	T	F
F	F	T

Note that $p \leftrightarrow q$ is true when p, q are both true or both false, and is false otherwise. As with the conditional $p \rightarrow q$ other wordings are common in mathematical literature. We tabulate some of the possibilities for future reference.

> p is equivalent to q
> q is equivalent to p
> if p then q, and if q then p
> if p then q, and conversely
> if q then p, and conversely
> p is necessary and sufficient for q
> q is necessary and sufficient for p
> q if and only if p

Example 5* Show that $p \leftrightarrow q = (p \rightarrow q) \wedge (q \rightarrow p)$.

That this is the case is obvious from the third of the possible variations above. It can also be verified by the truth table technique thus:

p	q	$p \rightarrow q$	$q \rightarrow p$	$(p \rightarrow q) \wedge (q \rightarrow p)$	$p \leftrightarrow q$
T	T	T	T	T	T
T	F	F	T	F	F
F	T	T	F	F	F
F	F	T	T	T	T

Example 6* Show that $p \leftrightarrow q = (p \wedge q) \vee (p' \wedge q')$.

Since $p \leftrightarrow q = (p \rightarrow q) \wedge (q \rightarrow p)$
$\qquad = (p' \vee q) \wedge (q' \vee p)$
$\qquad = (p' \wedge q') \vee (p' \wedge p) \vee (q \wedge q') \vee (q \wedge p)$
$\qquad = (p' \wedge q') \vee (q \wedge p)$
$\qquad = (p \wedge q) \vee (p' \wedge q')$

EXERCISES 3.6

1. Show that $p \rightarrow q = q' \rightarrow p'$.
2. What is the negation of (a) $p \rightarrow q$, (b) $p \leftrightarrow q$?
3. Show that the proposition $[(p \rightarrow q) \wedge (q \rightarrow r)] \rightarrow (q \rightarrow r)$ is a tautology.

4. Given that p is the proposition 'mathematicians are not practical men' and q is the proposition 'abstract thinkers enjoy using symbols', express in symbolic form the following propositions:

(a) That mathematicians are not practical men implies that abstract thinkers enjoy using symbols.

(b) Abstract thinkers enjoy using symbols only if mathematicians are not practical men.

(c) That mathematicians are not practical men is sufficient for abstract thinkers to enjoy using symbols.

(d) Some abstract thinkers do not enjoy using symbols if and only if mathematicians are practical men.

Chapter Four

INTRODUCTION TO MATRIX ALGEBRA

4.1 *Preliminary Ideas and Definitions*

A collection of numbers arranged in a rectangular table is called a *matrix*. It is important to realise that a matrix does *not* have a numerical value, but is merely an array of numbers.

Typical matrices are—

(a)
$$\begin{bmatrix} 5 & 3 \\ -1 & 6 \end{bmatrix}$$

(b)
$$\begin{bmatrix} 2 & 4 & -3 & -5 \\ 1 & -7 & 0 & 6 \\ 3 & 1 & 2 & -4 \end{bmatrix}$$

(c)
$$\begin{bmatrix} 1+i & -5+3i \\ 2i & -7 \end{bmatrix} \qquad (i^2 = -1)$$

(d)
$$\begin{bmatrix} 0 \\ -5 \\ 7 \\ 32 \end{bmatrix}$$

(e)
$$[1 \quad 3 \quad -2 \quad a^2+7 \quad 2b]$$

Matrices are usually denoted by capital letters A, B, C, D, . . . and a matrix with m rows and n columns is said to be an $m \times n$ matrix, or a matrix of order $m \times n$. When we say that two matrices A, B are of the *same order* we will mean that both matrices have the same number of rows, and also the same number of columns.

An $m \times m$ matrix, i.e. a matrix with the same number of rows and columns, is called a *square matrix of order m*.

A $1 \times m$ matrix, i.e. a matrix with only one row is called a *row matrix* or *row vector*.

An $m \times 1$ matrix, i.e. a matrix with only one column is called a *column matrix* or *column vector*.

Two matrices A, B are said to be *equal* if and only if they are of the same order and their corresponding elements are equal. If this is the case we will write A = B.

Example 1 $A = \begin{bmatrix} 2 & 1 & 5 \\ -5 & 0 & 7 \end{bmatrix}$ is a 2×3 matrix

Example 2 $B = \begin{bmatrix} 1 & 5 & 3 \\ -1 & 2 & 3 \\ 0 & 0 & 1 \\ 1 & 0 & 7 \end{bmatrix}$ is a 4×3 matrix

Example 3 $A = \begin{bmatrix} 1 & 7 \\ -1 & 0 \\ 12 & 5 \end{bmatrix}$ and $B = \begin{bmatrix} 2 & -5 \\ 6 & 7 \\ 1 & 2 \end{bmatrix}$

are both 3×2 matrices and hence are of the same order.

Example 4 $A = \begin{bmatrix} -1 & 2 & 3 \\ 0 & 7 & 5 \\ 2 & -1 & 6 \end{bmatrix}$

is a square matrix of order 3.

Example 5 $A = \begin{bmatrix} 3 & -1 & 2 & 5 & 6 \end{bmatrix}$

is a 1×5 row vector.

Example 6 $B = \begin{bmatrix} 0 \\ -1 \\ 0 \\ 2 \end{bmatrix}$

is a 4×1 column vector. This is sometimes written as $B = \{0 \ \ -1 \ \ 0 \ \ 2\}$ to economise in space.

Example 7* The general matrix of order 2 × 3 can be written

$$\begin{bmatrix} a_{11} & a_{12} & a_{13} \\ a_{21} & a_{22} & a_{23} \end{bmatrix}$$

Example 8* The general matrix of order $m \times n$ can be written

$$\begin{bmatrix} a_{11} & a_{12} & a_{13} \cdots a_{1n} \\ a_{21} & a_{22} & a_{23} \cdots a_{2n} \\ a_{31} & a_{32} & a_{33} \cdots a_{3n} \\ \cdot \\ \cdot \\ \cdot \\ a_{m1} & a_{m2} & a_{m3} \cdots a_{mn} \end{bmatrix}$$

Note that a_{ij} is the element contained in the ith row and in the jth column.

Example 9 If

$$A = \begin{bmatrix} -1 & 2 \\ 3 & 4 \end{bmatrix} \text{ and } B = \begin{bmatrix} -1 & 2 & 0 \\ 3 & 4 & 0 \end{bmatrix}$$

then $A \neq B$, since A is a 2 × 2 matrix and B is a 2 × 3 **matrix**.

Example 10 If

$$\begin{bmatrix} 3 & x & 2 \\ -1 & 0 & y \\ 7 & 5 & 6 \end{bmatrix} = \begin{bmatrix} 3 & -2 & 2 \\ -1 & 0 & 5 \\ 7 & 5 & 6 \end{bmatrix}$$

then $x = -2$ and $y = 5$.

Example 11 If

$$\begin{bmatrix} 3x - 2y + 4z \\ 5x + 2y - 3z \\ 7x + 5y - 2z \end{bmatrix} = \begin{bmatrix} 5 \\ 4 \\ 10 \end{bmatrix}$$

then

$$3x - 2y + 4z = 5$$
$$5x + 2y - 3z = 4$$
$$7x + 5y - 2z = 10$$

4.2 *Matrix Addition, Subtraction, and Scalar Multiplication*

Let A, B be two matrices of the *same* order. Then we define the *sum* of A and B to be the matrix, which is obtained by adding together corresponding elements of A and B, and we write it A + B. Similarly the *difference* between A and B is defined to be that matrix which is obtained by subtracting from each element of A the corresponding element of B, and it is written A − B.

Also if A is any matrix and k any scalar quantity we define kA to be the matrix which is obtained by multiplying each element of A by k.

Example 1   If

$$A = \begin{bmatrix} 3 & 1 & -5 \\ 2 & 1 & 6 \end{bmatrix} \text{ and } B = \begin{bmatrix} 5 & 2 & -4 \\ 0 & 7 & 6 \end{bmatrix}$$

then

$$A + B = \begin{bmatrix} 8 & 3 & -9 \\ 2 & 8 & 12 \end{bmatrix}$$

and

$$A - B = \begin{bmatrix} -2 & -1 & -1 \\ 2 & -6 & 0 \end{bmatrix}$$

Example 2   If

$$A = \begin{bmatrix} 3 & -5 & 6 \\ 2 & 1 & 5 \\ 0 & 7 & 4 \end{bmatrix} \text{ then } 3A = \begin{bmatrix} 9 & -15 & 18 \\ 6 & 3 & 15 \\ 0 & 21 & 12 \end{bmatrix}$$

Example 3   If

$$A = \begin{bmatrix} 5 & 1 \\ 2 & 7 \\ -3 & 4 \\ 1 & 6 \end{bmatrix} \text{ and } B = \begin{bmatrix} 4 & 2 \\ 0 & 1 \\ 3 & 2 \\ -1 & 6 \end{bmatrix}$$

then

$$3A - 2B = \begin{bmatrix} 15 & 3 \\ 6 & 21 \\ -9 & 12 \\ 3 & 18 \end{bmatrix} - \begin{bmatrix} 8 & 4 \\ 0 & 2 \\ 6 & 4 \\ -2 & 12 \end{bmatrix}$$

$$= \begin{bmatrix} 7 & -1 \\ 6 & 19 \\ -15 & 8 \\ 5 & 6 \end{bmatrix}$$

It is obvious that the operation of matrix addition on the set of all matrices of some given order is both commutative and associative, i.e. if A, B, C are three matrices of the same order then

$$A + B = B + A$$

and

$$A + (B + C) = (A + B) + C.$$

EXERCISES 4.2

1. If $A = \begin{bmatrix} 3 & -1 \\ 0 & 5 \end{bmatrix}$ and $B = \begin{bmatrix} 2 & -1 \\ -1 & 3 \end{bmatrix}$

evaluate the matrices $A + B$, $A - B$, $3A + 2B$, $A - 4B$.

2. If $A = \begin{bmatrix} 1 & -1 & 3 \\ 2 & 5 & -1 \\ 4 & 3 & 2 \end{bmatrix}$ and $B = \begin{bmatrix} 0 & 0 & -1 \\ 7 & 11 & 0 \\ 5 & -3 & 4 \end{bmatrix}$

evaluate the matrices $A + B$, $B - A$, $5A - B$, $2A + 3B$.

3. If $A = \begin{bmatrix} 2 - 3i \\ 3 + i \\ 5 - 2i \\ 3 + 2i \end{bmatrix}$, $B = \begin{bmatrix} 5 - i \\ 2 + 3i \\ 3 - 7i \\ 1 + i \end{bmatrix}$ and $C = \begin{bmatrix} 2 - 3i \\ 1 + 4i \\ -1 + 2i \\ 3 + 5i \end{bmatrix}$

evaluate the matrix $3A - 2B + C$.

4.3 *Diagonal, Scalar, Unit, and Null Matrices*

A *square* matrix of the form

$$\begin{bmatrix} a_{11} & 0 & 0 & \ldots & 0 \\ 0 & a_{22} & 0 & \ldots & 0 \\ 0 & 0 & a_{33} & \ldots & 0 \\ \cdot & & & & \\ \cdot & & & & \\ \cdot & & & & \\ 0 & 0 & 0 & \ldots & a_{nn} \end{bmatrix}$$

is called a *diagonal* matrix.

A *square* matrix of the form

$$\begin{bmatrix} \alpha & 0 & 0 & \ldots & 0 \\ 0 & \alpha & 0 & \ldots & 0 \\ 0 & 0 & \alpha & \ldots & 0 \\ \cdot & & & & \\ \cdot & & & & \\ \cdot & & & & \\ 0 & 0 & 0 & \ldots & \alpha \end{bmatrix}$$

is called a *scalar* matrix.

A *square* matrix of the form

$$\begin{bmatrix} 1 & 0 & 0 & \ldots & 0 \\ 0 & 1 & 0 & \ldots & 0 \\ 0 & 0 & 1 & \ldots & 0 \\ \cdot & & & & \\ \cdot & & & & \\ \cdot & & & & \\ 0 & 0 & 0 & \ldots & 1 \end{bmatrix}$$

is called a *unit* matrix and is denoted by the letter I (or I_n if the order of the unit matrix is important). Note that any scalar matrix is a scalar multiple of the unit matrix of the same order. Thus if

$$A = \begin{bmatrix} 3 & 0 & 0 \\ 0 & 3 & 0 \\ 0 & 0 & 3 \end{bmatrix}$$

then $A = 3I$ where

$$I = \begin{bmatrix} 1 & 0 & 0 \\ 0 & 1 & 0 \\ 0 & 0 & 1 \end{bmatrix}$$

A matrix of the form

$$\begin{bmatrix} 0 & 0 & 0 \ldots 0 \\ 0 & 0 & 0 \ldots 0 \\ 0 & 0 & 0 \ldots 0 \\ \cdot & & \\ \cdot & & \\ \cdot & & \\ 0 & 0 & 0 \ldots 0 \end{bmatrix}$$

is called a *null* matrix and is denoted by the symbol O. Note that O as used here is the symbol for a special matrix and not a number. If the order of the null matrix under consideration is important we may write $O_{m \times n}$.

Example 1 $A - A = O$ for all matrices A.

Example 2   O is a unit element for the operation of matrix addition, since $A + O = O + A = A$. We will show later that I_n is a unit element for matrix multiplication (which we have not yet defined) on the set of all $n \times n$ matrices.

4.4 *The Transpose of a Matrix: Symmetric and Skew-Symmetric Matrices*

The matrix A' of order $n \times m$, obtained by interchanging the rows and columns of an $m \times n$ matrix A, is called the transpose of A. (In some books $A^\top$ or $\tilde{A}$ are used instead of A'.)

Example 1   If $A = \begin{bmatrix} 3 & 2 & 1 & -5 \\ 6 & 1 & -2 & 7 \\ 5 & 0 & -4 & 8 \end{bmatrix}$

then $A' = \begin{bmatrix} 3 & 6 & 5 \\ 2 & 1 & 0 \\ 1 & -2 & -4 \\ -5 & 7 & 8 \end{bmatrix}$

Example 2* If A′, B′ are the transposes of A and B, and if α is any scalar, show that

> I. $(A')' = A$
>
> II. $(A + B)' = A' + B'$ (A, B of the same order)
>
> III. $(\alpha A)' = \alpha A'$

We will use the abbreviated notation $A = [a_{ij}]_{m,n}$ to mean that

$$A = \begin{bmatrix} a_{11} & a_{12} & a_{13} \ldots a_{1n} \\ a_{21} & a_{22} & a_{23} \ldots a_{2n} \\ \cdot \\ \cdot \\ \cdot \\ a_{m1} & a_{m2} & a_{m3} \ldots a_{mn} \end{bmatrix}$$

Proof of I   Let $A = [a_{ij}]_{m,n}$

Then $A' = [a_{ji}]_{n,m}$. (Note that this means that the element in the ith row and jth column of A′ is a_{ji}.)

$$\therefore \qquad (A')' = [a_{ij}]_{m,n}$$
$$= A$$
$$\therefore \qquad (A')' = A$$

Proof of II   Let $A = [a_{ij}]_{m,n}$ and $B = [b_{ij}]_{m,n}$

Then $\qquad\qquad A + B = [a_{ij} + b_{ij}]_{m,n}$
$$\therefore \qquad (A + B)' = [a_{ji} + b_{ji}]_{n,m}$$
$$= [a_{ji}]_{n,m} + [b_{ji}]_{n,m}$$
$$= A' + B'$$
$$\therefore \qquad (A + B)' = A' + B'$$

Proof of III   Let $A = [a_{ij}]_{m,n}$
$$\therefore \qquad\qquad \alpha A = [\alpha a_{ij}]_{m,n} \quad \text{(by Defn.)}$$
$$\therefore \qquad\qquad (\alpha A)' = [\alpha a_{ji}]_{n,m}$$
$$= \alpha [a_{ji}]_{n,m}$$
$$= \alpha A'$$
$$\therefore \qquad\qquad (\alpha A)' = \alpha A'$$

A *square* matrix A, such that $A' = A$, is said to be *symmetric*.

A *square* matrix A, such that $A' = -A$, is said to be *skew-symmetric*.

Example 3

The matrix $A = \begin{bmatrix} -2 & 5 & 6 \\ 5 & 7 & -3 \\ 6 & -3 & 8 \end{bmatrix}$ is symmetric.

Example 4

The matrix $A = \begin{bmatrix} a & h & g \\ h & b & f \\ g & f & c \end{bmatrix}$ is symmetric.

Example 5

The matrix $B = \begin{bmatrix} 0 & 5 & -3 & 6 \\ -5 & 0 & 7 & -4 \\ 3 & -7 & 0 & 1 \\ -6 & 4 & -1 & 0 \end{bmatrix}$ is skew-symmetric.

Example 6 Show that in a skew-symmetric matrix $A = [a_{ij}]_{n,n}$

$$\text{I. } a_{ii} = 0 \qquad i = 1, 2, 3, \ldots n$$
$$\text{II. } a_{ij} = -a_{ji} \qquad i \neq j$$

Since
$$A = [a_{ij}]_{n,n}$$
$$\therefore \qquad A' = [a_{ji}]_{n,n}$$

But $A' = -A$, since A is skew-symmetric.

$$\therefore \qquad [a_{ij}]_{n,n} = -[a_{ji}]_{n,n}$$
$$\therefore \qquad a_{ij} = -a_{ji}$$

Hence I. if $i = j$ $\quad a_{ii} = -a_{ii}$

$$\therefore \qquad a_{ii} = 0$$

II. if $i \neq j$ $\quad \underline{a_{ij} = -a_{ji}}$

EXERCISES 4.4

1. Verify that $(A + B)' = A' + B'$ in the case where

$$A = \begin{bmatrix} 1 & -1 & 2 \\ 3 & 1 & 4 \\ 2 & 3 & 0 \end{bmatrix} \text{ and } B = \begin{bmatrix} 3 & 0 & 5 \\ 2 & 1 & 3 \\ 0 & -1 & -7 \end{bmatrix}$$

2. If A is any square matrix show that $A + A'$ is symmetric and $A - A'$ skew-symmetric. Hence show that any square matrix A can be written in the form $B + C$, where B is a symmetric matrix and C a skew-symmetric matrix.

3. Write
$$A = \begin{bmatrix} 3 & 1 & 5 \\ 5 & 3 & 7 \\ 7 & 1 & 9 \end{bmatrix}$$

in the form $B + C$ where B is a symmetric matrix and C a skew-symmetric matrix.

4. Show that, in a symmetric matrix $A = [a_{ij}]$, $a_{ij} = a_{ji}$.

4.5 The Multiplication of Matrices

Let A be an $m \times p$ matrix and B an $p \times n$ matrix. Then the product AB is defined to be the $m \times n$ matrix C, whose element in the ith row and jth column is obtained *by multiplying together corresponding elements of the ith row of A and the jth column of B and adding the results.*
Symbolically if

$$A = [a_{ij}]_{m,p} \quad \text{and } B = [b_{ij}]_{p,n}$$
then $\qquad AB = [c_{ij}]_{m,n}$
where $\qquad c_{ij} = \sum_{k=1}^{k=p} a_{ik}b_{kj}$

Notes

I. AB is defined, if and only if the number of columns in A is the same as the number of rows in B. If this is the case A and B are said to be *conformable* for multiplication.

II. If AB is defined, then the number of rows in AB is the same as the number of rows in A, and the number of columns in AB is the same as the number of columns in B.

III. Notes I and II may be remembered by
(m, p) matrix $\times$ (p, n) matrix $= (m, n)$ matrix.

IV. AB and BA are both defined, if and only if A is an $m \times n$ matrix and B an $n \times m$ matrix.

V. Even when AB and BA are both defined, AB and BA are not equal in general. For if A is an $m \times n$ matrix and B an $n \times m$ matrix, the orders of AB and BA will be different, unless $m = n$. We will show later that even in the case where $m = n$, AB and BA are not necessarily equal.

VI. In the product AB we say that B is *premultiplied* by A, and that A is *post-multiplied* by B.

VII. If A, B are $m \times m$ matrices such that AB = BA, we say that A, B *commute*.

Example 1

$$\text{If} \quad A = \begin{bmatrix} 1 & -1 & 2 \\ 3 & 0 & 1 \end{bmatrix} \quad (2 \times 3)$$

$$B = \begin{bmatrix} 1 & 2 & 0 \\ 0 & -1 & 1 \\ 1 & 2 & -1 \end{bmatrix} \quad (3 \times 3)$$

then AB is the 2×3 matrix given by

$$AB = \begin{bmatrix} 3 & 7 & -3 \\ 4 & 8 & -1 \end{bmatrix}$$

For example the element in the 1st row and 3rd column of AB is obtained by multiplying corresponding elements of the 1st row of A and the 3rd column of B and then adding the results. Thus

$$(1)(0) + (-1)(1) + (2)(-1) = 0 - 1 - 2$$
$$= -3$$

Note that BA is not defined.

Example 2

$$\begin{bmatrix} 5 & -1 & 3 \\ 2 & 1 & 5 \\ 3 & -1 & 7 \end{bmatrix} \begin{bmatrix} x \\ y \\ z \end{bmatrix} = \begin{bmatrix} 5x - y + 3z \\ 2x + y + 5z \\ 3x - y + 7z \end{bmatrix}$$

$$(3 \times 3) \quad (3 \times 1) \qquad (3 \times 1)$$

Example 3 If $A = [5 \quad -3 \quad -7]$, $\quad B = \begin{bmatrix} -1 \\ 2 \\ 4 \end{bmatrix}$

then AB is the (1×1) matrix given by $AB = -39$ whereas BA is the (3×3) matrix given by

$$\begin{bmatrix} -5 & 3 & 7 \\ 10 & -6 & -14 \\ 20 & -12 & -28 \end{bmatrix}$$

Note that $AB \neq BA$.

Example 4 If

$$A = \begin{bmatrix} 1 & 0 & 3 \\ 3 & 5 & 7 \\ 0 & 1 & -1 \end{bmatrix}, \qquad B = \begin{bmatrix} 2 & 1 & 0 \\ -1 & 1 & 5 \\ 0 & 5 & 2 \end{bmatrix}$$

then

$$AB = \begin{bmatrix} 2 & 16 & 6 \\ 1 & 43 & 39 \\ -1 & -4 & 3 \end{bmatrix} \text{ whereas } BA = \begin{bmatrix} 5 & 5 & 13 \\ 2 & 10 & -1 \\ 15 & 27 & 33 \end{bmatrix}$$

Once again $AB \neq BA$.

Example 5

$$\text{If } A = \begin{bmatrix} 2 & 6 \\ -6 & 2 \end{bmatrix}, \quad B = \begin{bmatrix} 7 & -3 \\ 3 & 7 \end{bmatrix}$$

then

$$AB = \begin{bmatrix} 32 & 36 \\ -36 & 32 \end{bmatrix} = BA$$

In this case $AB = BA$, and therefore A and B commute.

Example 6 If A is any square matrix of order n and I is the unit matrix of the same order show that $IA = AI = A$. (Hence the name 'unit matrix'.)
   Let $A = [a_{ij}]_{n,n}$, then

$$IA = \begin{bmatrix} 1 & 0 & 0 & \dots 0 \\ 0 & 1 & 0 & \dots 0 \\ 0 & 0 & 1 & \dots 0 \\ \vdots \\ 0 & 0 & & \dots\dots 1 \end{bmatrix} \begin{bmatrix} a_{11} & a_{12} & a_{13} \dots a_{1n} \\ a_{21} & a_{22} & a_{23} \dots a_{2n} \\ \vdots \\ a_{n1} & a_{n2} & a_{n3} \dots a_{nn} \end{bmatrix}$$

$$= \begin{bmatrix} a_{11} & a_{12} & a_{13} \dots a_{1n} \\ a_{21} & a_{22} & a_{23} \dots a_{2n} \\ \cdot \\ \cdot \\ \cdot \\ a_{n1} & a_{n2} & a_{33} \dots a_{nn} \end{bmatrix}$$

$$= A.$$

Similarly $AI = A$.

$\therefore \ \underline{AI = IA = A.}$

Example 7 If

$$A = \begin{bmatrix} 1 & 2 & 0 \\ 1 & 1 & 0 \\ -1 & 4 & 0 \end{bmatrix}, \qquad B = \begin{bmatrix} 0 & 0 & 0 \\ 0 & 0 & 0 \\ 1 & 4 & 9 \end{bmatrix}$$

then $AB = \begin{bmatrix} 0 & 0 & 0 \\ 0 & 0 & 0 \\ 0 & 0 & 0 \end{bmatrix}$

$$= 0.$$

Hence although AB is null, neither A nor B is null.

Example 8 If $A = \begin{bmatrix} 1 & 2 & 0 \\ 1 & 1 & 0 \\ -1 & 4 & 0 \end{bmatrix}$

$$B = \begin{bmatrix} 1 & 2 & 3 \\ 1 & 1 & -1 \\ 2 & 2 & 2 \end{bmatrix}$$

$$C = \begin{bmatrix} 1 & 2 & 3 \\ 1 & 1 & -1 \\ 1 & 1 & 1 \end{bmatrix}$$

then $AB = \begin{bmatrix} 3 & 4 & 1 \\ 2 & 3 & 2 \\ 3 & 2 & -7 \end{bmatrix} = AC$

Hence we can have $AB = AC$ without it following that $B = C$.

EXERCISES 4.5

1. If $\quad A = \begin{bmatrix} 0 & 3 & -1 \\ -1 & 0 & 4 \\ 2 & 0 & -1 \end{bmatrix}$ and $B = \begin{bmatrix} 1 & -3 & 5 \\ 2 & 0 & -4 \\ 3 & 2 & 0 \end{bmatrix}$

evaluate the matrices AB, BA, A(BA) and (AB)A.

2. Perform the following matrix multiplications:

I.
$$\begin{bmatrix} 1 & -1 & 1 \\ 2 & 0 & 1 \\ 3 & -1 & 2 \end{bmatrix} \begin{bmatrix} 1 & 1 \\ -1 & 1 \\ 1 & 3 \end{bmatrix}$$

II. $[1 \quad 2 \quad 3 \quad 4] \quad \{1 \quad 2 \quad 3 \quad 4\}$

III. $\{1 \quad 2 \quad 3 \quad 4\} \quad [1 \quad 2 \quad 3 \quad 4]$

IV.
$$[2 \quad 1 \quad -1] \begin{bmatrix} 4 & -1 & 2 \\ -1 & 0 & 1 \\ 2 & 1 & 0 \end{bmatrix}$$

3. If $\quad A + I_3 = \begin{bmatrix} 1 & 2 & 5 \\ 3 & -1 & 2 \\ 3 & 1 & 0 \end{bmatrix}$

evaluate $(A + I_3)(A - I_3)$.

4. Show that the product of the two matrices

$$\begin{bmatrix} \cos^2 \theta & \cos \theta \sin \theta \\ \cos \theta \sin \theta & \sin^2 \theta \end{bmatrix}, \qquad \begin{bmatrix} \cos^2 \phi & \cos \phi \sin \phi \\ \cos \phi \sin \phi & \sin^2 \phi \end{bmatrix}$$

is null when θ and ϕ differ by an odd multiple of $\dfrac{\pi}{2}$.

4.6 The Laws of Matrix Multiplication

We have already seen that the operation of matrix multiplication is not in general commutative. That matrix multiplication is an associative operation and that it distributes over matrix addition can be proved. From now on we will assume that

I. $A(BC) \quad = (AB)C$

II. $A(B + C) = AB + AC$

III. $(B + C)A = BA + CA$

where A, B, C are matrices of the appropriate orders.

Example 1   Expand $(A + B)^2$

$$(A + B)^2 = (A + B)(A + B) = (A + B)A + (A + B)B$$
$$= AA + BA + AB + BB$$
$$= A^2 + BA + AB + B^2$$

(*N.B.* It is natural to define A^n, where n is a +ve integer, by

$A^n = A . A . A . . . . . A$ (n factors).)

EXERCISES 4.6

1. Verify that $A(BC) = (AB)C$ in the case where

$$A = \begin{bmatrix} 1 & -1 & 0 \\ 2 & 3 & 4 \end{bmatrix}, \quad B = \begin{bmatrix} 1 & 2 & 0 \\ 3 & 1 & 5 \\ -1 & 2 & -3 \end{bmatrix}, \quad C = \begin{bmatrix} 1 & 0 \\ 0 & 0 \\ 2 & -1 \end{bmatrix}.$$

2. Show that

$$\begin{bmatrix} x & y \end{bmatrix} \begin{bmatrix} a & h \\ h & b \end{bmatrix} \begin{bmatrix} x \\ y \end{bmatrix} = ax^2 + 2hxy + by^2$$

3. Show that $\begin{bmatrix} x & y & z \end{bmatrix} \begin{bmatrix} a & h & g \\ h & b & f \\ g & f & c \end{bmatrix} \begin{bmatrix} x \\ y \\ z \end{bmatrix}$

$$= ax^2 + by^2 + cz^2 + 2fyz + 2gzx + 2hxy$$

4. Show that

$$\begin{bmatrix} x & y & z \end{bmatrix} \begin{bmatrix} 0 & a & b \\ -a & 0 & c \\ -b & -c & 0 \end{bmatrix} \begin{bmatrix} x \\ y \\ z \end{bmatrix} = 0.$$

5. If A and B are square matrices of the same order, expand $(A - B)^2$ and $(A - B)^3$. Simplify your results if A and B commute.

6. If A and B are square matrices of the same order simplify

I. $(A + B) (A - B) - (A - B)(A + B)$

II. $(A + B)^3 + (A - B)^3 - 2A(A^2 + B^2)$

7. If $A = \begin{bmatrix} a_1 & b_1 \\ a_2 & b_2 \end{bmatrix}$

evaluate $A^2 - (a_1 + b_2)A + (a_1 b_2 - a_2 b_1)I$.

4.7 *The Transpose of a Product*

We will show that $(AB)' = B'A'$ where A is an $m \times p$ matrix and B a $p \times n$ matrix.

Let $A = [a_{ij}]_{m,p}$ and $B = [b_{ij}]_{p,n}$. Then $AB = [c_{ij}]_{m,n}$, where

$$c_{ij} = \sum_{k=1}^{k=p} a_{ik}b_{kj}$$

$\therefore (AB)' = [d_{ij}]_{n,m}$, where

$$d_{ij} = c_{ji}$$

$$= \sum_{k=1}^{k=p} a_{jk}b_{ki}$$

Also $B' = [x_{ij}]_{n,p}$, where $x_{ij} = b_{ji}$, and

$A' = [y_{ij}]_{p,m}$, where $y_{ij} = a_{ji}$

$\therefore B'A' = [z_{ij}]_{n,m}$, where $z_{ij} = \sum_{k=1}^{k=p} x_{ik}y_{kj}$

$$\therefore \quad z_{ij} = \sum_{k=1}^{k=p} x_{ik}y_{kj}$$

$$= \sum_{k=1}^{k=p} b_{ki}a_{jk}$$

$$= \sum_{k=1}^{k=p} a_{jk}b_{ki}$$

$$= d_{ij}$$

$\therefore \underline{(AB)' = B'A'}$

Example 1 Show that $(ABC)' = C'B'A'$.

$$(ABC)' = C'(AB)'$$
$$= C'(B'A')$$
$$= \underline{C'B'A'}$$

EXERCISES 4.7

1. Verify that $(AB)' = B'A'$ in the case where

$$A = \begin{bmatrix} 2 & -1 & 3 \\ 0 & 1 & 4 \end{bmatrix} \text{ and } B = \begin{bmatrix} 1 & 2 \\ 2 & 0 \\ -1 & 3 \end{bmatrix}$$

2. If A is any matrix show that the matrix AA' is symmetric.

3. A and B are square matrices of the same order and A is symmetric. Show that B'AB is symmetric.

4. A is an $n \times n$ skew-symmetric matrix and x is an $n \times 1$ column vector. Show that $x'Ax = 0$ (cf. No. 4, Exercises 4.6).

4.8 Linear Equations in Matrix Notation

The general system of m linear equations in n variables $x_1, x_2, x_3, \ldots x_n$ can be written

$$a_{11}x_1 + a_{12}x_2 + a_{13}x_3 + \ldots + a_{1n}x_n = b_1$$
$$a_{21}x_1 + a_{22}x_2 + a_{23}x_3 + \ldots + a_{2n}x_n = b_2$$

$$a_{m1}x_1 + a_{m2}x_2 + a_{m3}x_3 + \ldots + a_{mn}x_n = b_m$$

By the definition of matrix multiplication this set of equations can be written:

$$\begin{bmatrix} a_{11} & a_{12} & a_{13} \ldots a_{1n} \\ a_{21} & a_{22} & a_{23} \ldots a_{2n} \\ \cdot & & \cdot \\ \cdot & & \cdot \\ \cdot & & \cdot \\ a_{m1} & a_{m2} & a_{m3} \ldots a_{mn} \end{bmatrix} \begin{bmatrix} x_1 \\ x_2 \\ \cdot \\ \cdot \\ \cdot \\ x_n \end{bmatrix} = \begin{bmatrix} b_1 \\ b_2 \\ \cdot \\ \cdot \\ \cdot \\ b_m \end{bmatrix}$$

$$(m \times n) \qquad (n \times 1) \; (m \times 1)$$

Further, if we let

$$A = \begin{bmatrix} a_{11} & \cdot \, a_{12} & \ldots a_{1n} \\ a_{21} & a_{22} & \ldots a_{2n} \\ \cdot & \cdot & \cdot \\ \cdot & \cdot & \cdot \\ \cdot & \cdot & \cdot \\ a_{m1} & a_{m2} & \ldots a_{mn} \end{bmatrix}$$

$$x = \begin{bmatrix} x_1 \\ x_2 \\ . \\ . \\ . \\ x_n \end{bmatrix} \qquad b = \begin{bmatrix} b_1 \\ b_2 \\ . \\ . \\ . \\ b_m \end{bmatrix}$$

then this can be written in the highly compact form

$$Ax = b$$

A set of equations written in this form is said to be represented in *matrix notation*.

Example 1 Express the following set of simultaneous linear equations in matrix notation.

$$3x - 5y + 7z = -2$$
$$2x - 3y + 4z = 11 \; .$$
$$2x + 13y - 2z = 15$$

These can be written $Ax = b$, where

$$A = \begin{bmatrix} 3 & -5 & 7 \\ 2 & -3 & 4 \\ 2 & 13 & -2 \end{bmatrix} \qquad x = \begin{bmatrix} x \\ y \\ z \end{bmatrix} \qquad b = \begin{bmatrix} -2 \\ 11 \\ 15 \end{bmatrix}$$

Example 2   Given that

$$2x_1 + 3x_2 - 5x_3 = y_1$$
$$5x_1 - 2x_2 + 3x_3 = y_2$$
$$-2x_1 + 4x_2 - 3x_3 = y_3$$

and that

$$5y_1 - 3y_2 \qquad = z_1$$
$$6y_1 - y_2 + y_3 = z_2$$
$$y_1 + 4y_2 - y_3 - z_3$$

express the z's in terms of the x's.

We have that

$$Ax = y$$
$$By = z$$

....(1)

where

$$A = \begin{bmatrix} 2 & 3 & -5 \\ 5 & -2 & 3 \\ -2 & 4 & -3 \end{bmatrix} \qquad B = \begin{bmatrix} 5 & -3 & 0 \\ 6 & -1 & 1 \\ 1 & 4 & -1 \end{bmatrix}$$

$$x = \begin{bmatrix} x_1 \\ x_2 \\ x_3 \end{bmatrix} \qquad y = \begin{bmatrix} y_1 \\ y_2 \\ y_3 \end{bmatrix} \qquad z = \begin{bmatrix} z_1 \\ z_2 \\ z_3 \end{bmatrix}$$

From (1)
$$\begin{aligned} z &= By \\ &= B(Ax) \\ &= (BA)x \end{aligned}$$

Now
$$BA = \begin{bmatrix} -5 & 21 & -34 \\ 5 & 24 & -36 \\ 24 & -9 & 10 \end{bmatrix}$$

$$\therefore \quad \begin{aligned} z_1 &= -5x_1 + 21x_2 - 34x_3 \\ z_2 &= 5x_1 + 24x_2 - 36x_3 \\ z_3 &= 24x_1 - 9x_2 + 10x_3 \end{aligned}$$

EXERCISES 4.8

1. Given that

$$\begin{aligned} y_1 &= 2x_1 - 3x_2 \\ y_2 &= x_1 + 5x_2 \end{aligned} \Big\} \text{ and } \begin{aligned} x_1 &= 2u_1 + 6u_2 \\ x_2 &= 5u_1 - 2u_2 \end{aligned} \Big\}$$

express y_1 and y_2 in terms of u_1 and u_2.

2. Given that

$$\begin{aligned} u_1 &= 5v_1 + v_2 \\ u_2 &= 3v_1 - v_2 \end{aligned}\Big\}, \quad \begin{aligned} x_1 &= 2u_1 - 3u_2 \\ x_2 &= u_1 + 4u_2 \end{aligned}\Big\}, \quad \begin{aligned} y_1 &= 2x_1 - 3x_2 \\ y_2 &= 3x_1 - x_2 \end{aligned}\Big\}$$

express y_1 and y_2 in terms of v_1 and v_2.

4.9 Revision of Determinantal Theory

It is assumed that the reader is already familiar with the elementary theory of determinants. Some of their more important properties are outlined here, mainly without proof.

2×2 *Determinants*

$$\begin{vmatrix} a_{11} & a_{12} \\ a_{21} & a_{22} \end{vmatrix} = a_{11}a_{22} - a_{12}a_{21}$$

3×3 *Determinants*

$$\begin{vmatrix} a_{11} & a_{12} & a_{13} \\ a_{21} & a_{22} & a_{23} \\ a_{31} & a_{32} & a_{33} \end{vmatrix}$$

$$= a_{11} \begin{vmatrix} a_{22} & a_{23} \\ a_{32} & a_{33} \end{vmatrix} - a_{12} \begin{vmatrix} a_{21} & a_{23} \\ a_{31} & a_{33} \end{vmatrix} + a_{13} \begin{vmatrix} a_{21} & a_{22} \\ a_{31} & a_{32} \end{vmatrix}$$

etc.

Example 1

$$\begin{vmatrix} 5 & 7 & -3 \\ 2 & 5 & -1 \\ 6 & 0 & 5 \end{vmatrix} = 5 \begin{vmatrix} 5 & -1 \\ 0 & 5 \end{vmatrix} - 7 \begin{vmatrix} 2 & -1 \\ 6 & 5 \end{vmatrix} - 3 \begin{vmatrix} 2 & 5 \\ 6 & 0 \end{vmatrix}$$

$$= 5(25 + 0) - 7(10 + 6) - 3(0 - 30)$$
$$= 125 - 112 + 90$$
$$= \underline{103}$$

It can be shown that it is not essential to use the elements in the first row, when expanding a determinant. The elements in any row or column will serve equally well provided that, if a_{ij} is an element in the row or column selected, *it is multiplied by* $(-1)^{i+j}$.

Example 2
$$\Delta = \begin{vmatrix} 2 & 1 & 3 \\ 4 & 1 & 2 \\ 1 & 1 & 5 \end{vmatrix}$$

I. Expanding down first column

$$\Delta = (-1)^{1+1} . 2 . \begin{vmatrix} 1 & 2 \\ 1 & 5 \end{vmatrix} + (-1)^{2+1} . 4 . \begin{vmatrix} 1 & 3 \\ 1 & 5 \end{vmatrix}$$

$$+ (-1)^{3+1} . 1 . \begin{vmatrix} 1 & 3 \\ 1 & 2 \end{vmatrix}$$

$$= 2(3) - 4(2) + 1(-1)$$
$$= \underline{-3}$$

II. Expanding along second row

$$\Delta = (-1)^{2+1} . 4 \begin{vmatrix} 1 & 3 \\ 1 & 5 \end{vmatrix} + (-1)^{2+2} . 1 \begin{vmatrix} 2 & 3 \\ 1 & 5 \end{vmatrix}$$

$$+ (-1)^{2+3} . 2 \begin{vmatrix} 2 & 1 \\ 1 & 1 \end{vmatrix}$$

$$= -4(2) + 1(7) - 2(1)$$
$$= \underline{-3} \text{ (as before).}$$

Example 3   Evaluate $= \begin{vmatrix} a & a & b \\ 1 & b & a \\ a & 0 & 0 \end{vmatrix}$

Expanding along third row

$$= (-1)^{3+1} . a . \begin{vmatrix} a & b \\ b & a \end{vmatrix}$$

$$= \underline{a(a^2 - b^2)}$$

4×4 *determinants* are similarly evaluated.

Example 4   Evaluate $= \begin{vmatrix} 2 & 3 & 1 & 2 \\ 3 & 2 & 0 & 2 \\ 1 & 0 & 5 & 1 \\ 3 & 0 & 1 & 1 \end{vmatrix}$

Expanding down the second column

$$A = (-1)^{1+2} . 3 . \begin{vmatrix} 3 & 0 & 2 \\ 1 & 5 & 1 \\ 3 & 1 & 1 \end{vmatrix} + (-1)^{2+2} . 2 . \begin{vmatrix} 3 & 1 & 2 \\ 1 & 5 & 1 \\ 3 & 1 & 1 \end{vmatrix}$$

$$= -3(-16) + 2(-18)$$
$$= \underline{12}$$

Properties of Determinants

N.B. We shall use the word *line* to signify either a row or a column.

P.1   The value of a determinant is unaltered if rows and columns are interchanged.

P.2   If two parallel lines of a determinant Δ, are interchanged to yield a new determinant Δ', then $\Delta = -\Delta'$.

P.3   If two parallel lines of a determinant are equal then the value of the determinant is zero.

P.4   If all the elements in *one* line of a determinant are multiplied (or divided) by a constant λ, then the value of the determinant is also multiplied (or divided) by λ.

P.5   The value of a determinant is unaltered by adding to the elements in any line or parallel lines, positive or negative multiples of the corresponding elements in any other parallel line or lines *provided* at least one line is left unaltered at the end of the process.

Example 5

$$\begin{vmatrix} 14 & 7 & 4 \\ 5 & 2 & 3 \\ 6 & 3 & 3 \end{vmatrix} = \begin{vmatrix} 0 & 3 & 4 \\ 1 & -1 & 3 \\ 0 & 0 & 3 \end{vmatrix} \quad \begin{aligned} c_1' &= c_1 - 2c_2 \\ c_2' &= c_2 - c_3 \end{aligned}$$

$$= -1(9 - 0)$$
$$= -9$$

Example 6

$$\begin{vmatrix} 7 & 13 & 10 & 6 \\ 5 & 9 & 7 & 4 \\ 8 & 12 & 11 & 7 \\ 4 & 10 & 6 & 3 \end{vmatrix} = \begin{vmatrix} 3 & 3 & 4 & 3 \\ 5 & 9 & 7 & 4 \\ 3 & 3 & 4 & 3 \\ 4 & 10 & 6 & 3 \end{vmatrix} \quad \begin{aligned} r_1' &= r_1 - r_4 \\ r_3' &= r_3 - r_2 \end{aligned}$$

$$= 0$$

Minors and Cofactors

Given
$$\Delta = \begin{vmatrix} a_{11} & a_{12} & a_{13} \ldots a_{1n} \\ a_{21} & a_{22} & a_{23} \ldots a_{2n} \\ a_{31} & a_{32} & a_{33} \ldots a_{3n} \\ \cdot & & \\ \cdot & & \\ \cdot & & \\ a_{n1} & a_{n2} & a_{n3} \ldots a_{nn} \end{vmatrix}$$

we define the *minor* of an element a_{ij} to be the determinant formed by the elements of Δ which are left when the elements in the row and column containing a_{ij} have been deleted. We also define the *cofactor* of any element a_{ij} to be the minor of a_{ij} multiplied by $(-1)^{i+j}$. It is customary to denote the cofactor of an element a_{ij} in the determinant Δ by A_{ij}.

Example 7   If $= \begin{vmatrix} 5 & -1 & 2 & -7 \\ 6 & -2 & 1 & 3 \\ 4 & -4 & 9 & -5 \\ 0 & -6 & 7 & -8 \end{vmatrix}$

then I the minor of a_{32} (i.e. -4) is

$$\begin{vmatrix} 5 & 2 & -7 \\ 6 & 1 & 3 \\ 0 & 7 & -8 \end{vmatrix}$$

II   the cofactor of a_{41} (i.e. 0) is

$$(-1)^{4+1} \begin{vmatrix} -1 & 2 & -7 \\ -2 & 1 & 3 \\ -4 & 9 & -5 \end{vmatrix}$$

Properties of Cofactors

Given $\Delta = \begin{vmatrix} a_{11} & a_{12} & a_{13} \ldots a_{1n} \\ a_{21} & a_{22} & a_{23} \ldots a_{2n} \\ \cdot \\ \cdot \\ \cdot \\ a_{n1} & a_{n2} & a_{n3} \ldots a_{nn} \end{vmatrix}$

then

P.6   If each element in any line of Δ is multiplied by its cofactor and then the results added, the sum formed is equal to the value of Δ.

Symbolically:

$$\text{I. } a_{i1}A_{i1} + a_{i2}A_{i2} + \ldots + a_{in}A_{in} = \Delta$$
$$\text{II. } a_{1j}A_{1j} + a_{2j}A_{2j} + \ldots + a_{nj}A_{nj} = \Delta$$
$$(i, j = 1, 2, 3, \ldots n)$$

P.7   If each element in any line of Δ is multiplied by the cofactor of the corresponding element in some other parallel line of Δ and then the results added, the sum formed is equal to zero. (This is the theorem of 'false cofactors'.)

Symbolically:

$$\text{I. } a_{i1}A_{j1} + a_{i2}A_{j2} + \ldots + a_{in}A_{jn} = 0$$

$$\text{II. } a_{1i}A_{1j} + a_{2i}A_{2j} + \ldots + a_{ni}A_{nj} = 0$$

$$(i \neq j)$$

Example 8 Consider $\Delta = \begin{vmatrix} a & h & g \\ h & b & f \\ g & f & c \end{vmatrix}$

The elements of the first column are a, h, g.

The cofactors of elements of second column are:

$$- \begin{vmatrix} h & f \\ g & c \end{vmatrix}, \quad \begin{vmatrix} a & g \\ g & c \end{vmatrix}, \quad - \begin{vmatrix} a & g \\ h & f \end{vmatrix}$$

Now $S = - a(hc - gf) + h(ac - g^2) - g(af - gh)$

$$= - ach + afg + ach - g^2h - afg + g^2h$$

$$= 0 \text{ (as expected)}.$$

4.10 *The Determinant of a Square Matrix*

Given a *square* matrix A, say

$$A = \begin{bmatrix} a_{11} & a_{12} \ldots a_{1n} \\ a_{21} & a_{22} \ldots a_{2n} \\ \cdot \\ \cdot \\ \cdot \\ a_{n1} & a_{n2} \ldots a_{nn} \end{bmatrix}$$

then we define the determinant of the matrix A to be $|A|$ where

$$|A| = \begin{vmatrix} a_{11} & a_{12} \ldots a_{1n} \\ a_{21} & a_{22} \ldots a_{2n} \\ \cdot \\ \cdot \\ \cdot \\ a_{n1} & a_{n2} \ldots a_{nn} \end{vmatrix}$$

A square matrix A is said to be *singular* if $|A| = 0$. Also if A and B are two square matrices of the same order it can be shown that $|AB| = |A|\,|B|$.

Example 1 Verify that $|AB| = |A|\,|B|$ when

$$A = \begin{bmatrix} 1 & 2 & 3 \\ 3 & -1 & 4 \\ 2 & 0 & 5 \end{bmatrix} \text{ and } B = \begin{bmatrix} -1 & 0 & 2 \\ 1 & 0 & 2 \\ 5 & 1 & 2 \end{bmatrix}$$

Here

$$AB = \begin{bmatrix} 16 & 3 & 12 \\ 16 & 4 & 12 \\ 23 & 5 & 14 \end{bmatrix}$$

$\therefore\ |A| = -13,\ |B| = 4,\ |AB| = -52.$

$\therefore\ \underline{|AB| = |A|\,|B|}$

Example 2 If $AB = 0$, show that either A or B is singular (or both).

Since $\qquad\qquad AB = 0$

$\therefore \qquad\qquad |AB| = 0$

$\therefore \qquad\qquad |A|\,|B| = 0$

$\therefore \qquad\qquad |A| = 0$ or $|B| = 0$ or both.

EXERCISES 4.10

1. Verify that $|AB| = |A|\,|B|$ in the case where

$$A = \begin{bmatrix} 1 & 2 & 3 \\ -1 & 2 & 0 \\ 3 & 1 & 2 \end{bmatrix} \text{ and } B = \begin{bmatrix} 5 & 0 & -1 \\ 2 & 1 & 3 \\ 4 & 1 & -2 \end{bmatrix}$$

2.* Show that if α is a scalar and A a square matrix of order n, then

$$|\alpha A| = \alpha^n |A|$$

3. Show that the product of the matrices

$$\begin{bmatrix} a + ib & c + id \\ -c + id & a - ib \end{bmatrix} \text{ and } \begin{bmatrix} x - iy & u - iv \\ -u - iv & x + iy \end{bmatrix}$$

is of the form

$$\begin{bmatrix} \alpha - i\beta & \gamma - i\delta \\ -\gamma - i\delta & \alpha + i\beta \end{bmatrix}$$

where $i^2 = -1$ and $a, b, c, d, x, y, u, v, \alpha, \beta, \gamma, \delta$ are real. Deduce by taking determinants that the product of two numbers each of which is the sum of four squares can also be expressed as the sum of four squares.

4.11 *The Inverse of a Matrix*

Given a *square* matrix A, if there exists a matrix B such that $AB = BA = I$, then we say that B is the inverse matrix to A.

Lemma 1 A singular matrix A has no inverse.

Proof Assume that A has an inverse B.
  Then $AB = I$
  $\therefore$ $\qquad\qquad\qquad |AB| = 1$
  $\therefore$ $\qquad\qquad\qquad |A|\,|B| = 1$ $\qquad\qquad$ ....(1)
But $|A| = 0$ since A is singular, contradicting (1).
  Hence a singular matrix A has no inverse.

Lemma 2 The inverse of a non-singular square matrix A is unique. (That is given a non-singular square matrix A *there is at most only one matrix B* such that $AB = BA = I$.)

Proof Assume that A has two inverses B, C. Then $AB = BA = I$ and $AC = CA = I$.
  Hence $\qquad\qquad\qquad CAB = C$
  But $\qquad\qquad\qquad CA = I$
  $\therefore$ $\qquad\qquad\qquad IB = C$
  $\therefore$ $\qquad\qquad\qquad B = C$
Hence the inverse of a non-singular matrix A is unique.

N.B.   Since the inverse of a non-singular matrix is unique, if it exists, we can designate it by a suitable symbol. The usual choice is A^{-1}.
  Thus $\qquad\qquad AA^{-1} = A^{-1}A = I$

4.12 *The Adjugate Matrix*

Let $A = [a_{ij}]$ be a square matrix. Then we define the *adjugate matrix* of A, written adj. A, by

$$\text{adj } A = [A_{ij}]'$$

i.e. to form adj A we replace each element of A by its cofactor in $|A|$ and then transpose the resulting matrix.

Example 1   If
$$A = \begin{bmatrix} 1 & 1 & 0 \\ 2 & 3 & -1 \\ 0 & 5 & -1 \end{bmatrix}$$

then
$$[A_{ij}] = \begin{bmatrix} 2 & 2 & 10 \\ 1 & -1 & -5 \\ -1 & 1 & 1 \end{bmatrix}$$

$\therefore$
$$\text{adj } A = [A_{ij}]' = \begin{bmatrix} 2 & 1 & -1 \\ 2 & -1 & 1 \\ 10 & -5 & 1 \end{bmatrix}$$

The importance of the adjugate matrix of A is embodied in the following theorem.

Theorem   If A is a non-singular square matrix then

$$A(\text{adj } A) = (\text{adj } A)A = |A|I.$$

Proof   We shall show that $A(\text{adj } A) = |A|I$. The proof that $(\text{adj } A)A = |A|I$ is similar

let
$$A = \begin{bmatrix} a_{11} & a_{12} & a_{13} \ldots a_{1n} \\ a_{21} & a_{22} & a_{23} \ldots a_{2n} \\ . \\ . \\ . \\ a_{n1} & a_{n2} & a_{n3} \ldots a_{nn} \end{bmatrix}$$

Then
$$\text{adj } A = \begin{bmatrix} A_{11} & A_{21} & A_{31} \ldots A_{n1} \\ A_{12} & A_{22} & A_{32} \ldots A_{n2} \\ . \\ . \\ . \\ A_{1n} & A_{2n} & A_{3n} \ldots A_{nn} \end{bmatrix}$$

Hence $\quad A\,(\text{adj }A) = \begin{bmatrix} C_{11} & C_{12} & C_{13} & \ldots & C_{1n} \\ C_{21} & C_{22} & C_{23} & \ldots & C_{2n} \\ \cdot & & & & \\ \cdot & & & & \\ \cdot & & & & \\ C_{n1} & C_{n2} & C_{n3} & \ldots & C_{nn} \end{bmatrix}$

where $\quad C_{ij} = a_{i1}A_{j1} + a_{i2}A_{j2} + a_{i3}A_{i3} + \ldots + a_{in}A_{jn}$

$\therefore \qquad \left. \begin{array}{l} C_{ij} = |A| \text{ if } i = j \\ \quad\ 0 \ \ \text{ if } i \neq j \end{array} \right\}$ using P.6 and P.7

of the properties of determinants.

Hence $A\,(\text{adj }A) =$

$$\begin{bmatrix} |A| & 0 & 0 & \ldots & 0 \\ 0 & |A| & 0 & \ldots & 0 \\ \cdot & & & & \\ \cdot & & & & \\ \cdot & & & & \\ 0 & 0 & 0 & \ldots & |A| \end{bmatrix}$$

$$= |A| \begin{bmatrix} 1 & 0 & 0 & \ldots & 0 \\ 0 & 1 & 0 & \ldots & 0 \\ \cdot & & & & \\ \cdot & & & & \\ \cdot & & & & \\ 0 & 0 & 0 & \ldots & 1 \end{bmatrix}$$

$$= |A|I$$

$\therefore \qquad \underline{A\,(\text{adj }A) = |A|I}$

N.B.* It follows immediately that

$$A\left(\frac{1}{|A|} \text{ adj } A\right) = \left(\frac{1}{|A|} \text{ adj } A\right) A = I$$

Hence $\dfrac{1}{|A|}$ adj A is the inverse matrix of A.

Hence $\underline{A^{-1} = \dfrac{1}{|A|} \text{ adj } A}$

Example 2   Find the inverse of

$$A = \begin{bmatrix} 8 & 4 & 2 \\ 2 & 8 & 4 \\ 1 & 2 & 8 \end{bmatrix}$$

We have to determine $\dfrac{1}{|A|}$ adj A. This is best done in the following steps:

I. Evaluate $|A|$.

II. Replace each element of A by its cofactor.

III. Transpose the resulting matrix.

IV. Divide each element of this new matrix by $|A|$.

Thus in the above case

I. $|A| = 8(56) - 4(12) + 2(-4) = 392$.

II.
$$[A_{ij}] = \begin{bmatrix} 56 & -12 & -4 \\ -28 & 62 & -12 \\ 0 & -28 & 56 \end{bmatrix}$$

III.
$$\text{adj } A = \begin{bmatrix} 56 & -28 & 0 \\ -12 & 62 & -28 \\ -4 & -12 & 56 \end{bmatrix}$$

IV. $A^{-1} = \dfrac{1}{|A|}$ adj A =

$$\begin{bmatrix} \dfrac{1}{7} & -\dfrac{1}{14} & 0 \\ -\dfrac{3}{98} & \dfrac{31}{196} & -\dfrac{1}{14} \\ -\dfrac{1}{98} & -\dfrac{3}{98} & \dfrac{1}{7} \end{bmatrix}$$

Example 3   Solve for x, y, z

$$x + 2y + z = 4$$
$$x - y + z = 5$$
$$2x + 3y - z = 1$$

These equations can be written $Ax = b$, where

$$A = \begin{bmatrix} 1 & 2 & 1 \\ 1 & -1 & 1 \\ 2 & 3 & -1 \end{bmatrix} \quad x = \begin{bmatrix} x \\ y \\ z \end{bmatrix} \quad b = \begin{bmatrix} 4 \\ 5 \\ 1 \end{bmatrix}$$

Hence premultiplying both sides of $Ax = b$ by A^{-1} we obtain

$$A^{-1}Ax = A^{-1}b$$

$$\therefore \qquad x = A^{-1}b$$

Now $|A| = 9$ and hence $A^{-1} = \dfrac{1}{9} \begin{bmatrix} -2 & 5 & 3 \\ 3 & -3 & 0 \\ 5 & 1 & -3 \end{bmatrix}$

$$\therefore \qquad \begin{bmatrix} x \\ y \\ z \end{bmatrix} = \frac{1}{9} \begin{bmatrix} -2 & 5 & 3 \\ 3 & -3 & 0 \\ 5 & 1 & -3 \end{bmatrix} \begin{bmatrix} 4 \\ 5 \\ 1 \end{bmatrix}$$

$$= \frac{1}{9} \begin{bmatrix} 20 \\ -3 \\ 22 \end{bmatrix}$$

$$\therefore \quad x = \frac{20}{9}, y = \frac{-1}{3}, z = \frac{22}{9}$$

EXERCISES 4.12

1. Find the inverses of the following matrices

$$\text{I} \begin{bmatrix} 1 & 3 \\ -1 & 4 \end{bmatrix} \qquad \text{II} \begin{bmatrix} 3x & -4y \\ 4x & 5y \end{bmatrix}$$

$$\text{III} \begin{bmatrix} 1 & 0 & 2 \\ 3 & 4 & 1 \\ -6 & 3 & 5 \end{bmatrix} \qquad \text{IV} \begin{bmatrix} 5 & 2 & -4 \\ 3 & 2 & 4 \\ 2 & -1 & 6 \end{bmatrix}$$

2. Solve for x, y, z by matrix methods

$$x + y + z = 1$$
$$2x - y + 2z = -1$$
$$x + 3y + 2z = 2$$

3. If
$$A = \begin{bmatrix} 1 & -3 & 0 \\ 2 & 0 & 1 \\ 4 & 1 & 3 \end{bmatrix}$$

find A^{-1} and hence solve the equations

$$\begin{aligned} x - 3y \quad\quad &= a \\ 2x \quad\quad + z &= b \\ 4x + y + 3z &= c \end{aligned}$$

for x, y, z in terms of a, b, c.

4.13 The Inverse of the Product of Two Matrices

Theorem Let A, B be two non-singular square matrices of the same order. Then $(AB)^{-1} = B^{-1}A^{-1}$.

Proof Let
$$C = (AB)^{-1}$$
$$\therefore \quad\quad CAB = I$$
$$\therefore \quad\quad CAB\,B^{-1} = B^{-1}$$
$$\therefore \quad\quad CA = B^{-1}$$
$$\therefore \quad\quad CAA^{-1} = B^{-1}A^{-1}$$
$$\therefore \quad\quad C = B^{-1}A^{-1}$$
$$\therefore \quad\quad (AB)^{-1} = B^{-1}A^{-1}$$

EXERCISES 4.13

1. Verify that $(AB)^{-1} = B^{-1}A^{-1}$ in the case where
$$A = \begin{bmatrix} 3 & 1 \\ 4 & -5 \end{bmatrix} \quad\quad B = \begin{bmatrix} -1 & 5 \\ 2 & 1 \end{bmatrix}$$

2. Show that $(ABC)^{-1} = C^{-1}B^{-1}A^{-1}$ and generalise the result.

3. Given that
$$A = \begin{bmatrix} \dfrac{1}{3} & \dfrac{2}{3} & -\dfrac{2}{3} \\[2mm] \dfrac{14}{15} & -\dfrac{1}{3} & \dfrac{2}{15} \\[2mm] \dfrac{2}{15} & \dfrac{2}{3} & \dfrac{11}{15} \end{bmatrix}$$

verify that (a) $|A| = -1$, (b) $AA' = I$ and write down A^{-1}.

Chapter Five

GROUPS

5.1

One of the most important (and simplest) of abstract mathematical structures is a *group*. A set of elements $G = \{a, b, c, \ldots\}$ under an operation $*$ is said to form a group if the following postulates are satisfied.

1. *Closure Property of G*

   $*$ is a *binary* operation, i.e. if $a, b \in G$ then $a * b \in G$.

2. *Associative Law in G*

   $a * (b * c) = (a * b) * c$ for all $a, b, c \in G$.

3. *Existence of an Identity Element in G*

   There is an element $e \in G$ such that

   $$a * e = e * a = a \text{ for every } a \in G.$$

4. *Existence of an Inverse in G*

   For each $a \in G$ there exists an element $a^{-1} \in G$ such that

   $$a * a^{-1} = a^{-1} * a = e$$

   a^{-1} is called the *inverse* of the element a.

   Note that

   (*a*) We shall quite often omit the binary operation symbol $*$ when no confusion can arise by doing so. Thus the associative law may be written $a(bc) = (ab)c$ for all $a, b, c \in G$.

   (*b*) If the elements of a group G also satisfy the additional condition that $ab = ba$ for all $a, b \in G$ then we shall say that the group G is *Abelian*.

   (*c*) The identity element e is unique. For if e_1 and e_2 are both identity elements then

   $e_1 e_2 = e_2$ since e_1 is an identity element and
   $e_1 e_2 = e_1$ since e_2 is an identity element

   Hence $e_1 = e_2$.

(d) The inverse of an element $a \in G$ is unique. For if a has two inverses x, y then

$$ax = xa = e \qquad \dots (1)$$

and

$$ay = ya = e \qquad \dots (2)$$

Now using (1) $yax = ye$

∴ $yax = y$

and using (2) $yax = ex$

∴ $yax = x$

Hence $x = y$.

(e) It follows immediately from (d) that if a, b are elements of a group G, then the equation $ax = b$ has a unique solution in G. For premultiplying both sides of the equation by a^{-1} (which is unique) we have that

$$a^{-1} ax = a^{-1}b$$

∴ $x = a^{-1}b$

(f) We shall write, just as in ordinary algebra, a^2 for aa, a^3 for aaa, etc. It is not difficult to show that

$$a^m a^n = a^n a^m = a^{m+n}$$

and

$$(a^m)^n = a^{mn}$$

where m, n are positive integers.

(g) The number of elements in a group G may be finite or infinite. If a finite group G contains n elements then we shall say that the group G is of *order n*.

Example 1 The set I of all integers under the operation of addition is a group. For

I. The operation of addition on the set I is a binary operation.

II. $a + (b + c) = (a + b) + c$ for all $a, b, c \in I$.

III. $a + 0 = 0 + a = a$ for every $a \in I$ so that 0 is the identity element.

IV. $a + (-a) = (-a) + a = 0$ for every $a \in I$ so that each element $a \in I$ has a unique inverse $(-a) \in I$.

(Note the change in notation to avoid confusion.)

Example 2   The set R of all rational numbers with zero excluded is a group under the operation of multiplication. For

I. The operation of multiplication on the set R is a binary operation.

II. $a(bc) = (ab)c$ for all $a, b, c, \in$ R.

III. $a \cdot 1 = 1 \cdot a = a$ for every $a \in$ R so that 1 is the identity element.

IV. $a \cdot \dfrac{1}{a} = \dfrac{1}{a} \cdot a = 1$ for every $a \in$ R so that each element $a \in$ R has a unique inverse $\dfrac{1}{a} \in$ R.

Note that 0 must be excluded, for 0 has no inverse in the set of all rational numbers under the operation of multiplication.

Example 3   The set I of all integers under the operation of multiplication is not a group.

For if $a \in$ I, a may not have an inverse $a^{-1} \in$ I. For example, $2 \in$ I but there is no element $x \in$ I such that $2 \cdot x = x \cdot 2 = 1$.

Example 4   The set K whose elements are the matrices

$$I = \begin{bmatrix} 1 & 0 \\ 0 & 1 \end{bmatrix}, \qquad A = \begin{bmatrix} -1 & 0 \\ 0 & -1 \end{bmatrix}, \qquad B = \begin{bmatrix} 0 & 1 \\ -1 & 0 \end{bmatrix},$$

$$C = \begin{bmatrix} 0 & -1 \\ 1 & 0 \end{bmatrix}$$

is a group under the operation of matrix multiplication. For

I. by performing the necessary matrix multiplications it is easy to show that the operation of matrix multiplication on the elements of K is a binary operation,

II. By the associative property of matrix multiplication $a(bc) = (ab)c$ for all $a, b, c \in$ K,

III. $I \cdot a = a \cdot I = a$ for every $a \in$ K so that I is the identity element,

IV. It is easy to verify that

$$A^2 = BC = CB = I$$

so that I, A, B, C have the respective inverses I, A, C and B.

Example 5 The rules of combination of a set of elements a, b, c, . . . under an operation $*$ are often displayed in a 'multiplication' table. Consider, for example, a possible 'multiplication' table for the set of elements e, a, b, c under the operation $*$, namely

$*$	e	a	b	c
e	e	a	b	c
a	a	e	c	b
b	b	c	e	a
c	c	b	a	e

(To find $b * a$, for example, we take the element which is at the point of intersection of the row labelled b with the column labelled a, i.e. $b * a = c$. Similarly $a * c = b$, $c * a = b$, $e * a = a$, etc.)

The question naturally arises—is the set of elements e, a, b, c under the operation $*$, as defined by the above table, a group? That the answer is in the affirmative in this case can be established by verifying that the above system satisfies the group postulates.

I. That $*$ is a binary operation follows from the fact that every element in the body of the table is e, a, b or c.

II. That the associative law holds in the above system is not difficult (but rather tedious) to establish. For example

$$a * (b * c) = a * a = e$$
$$(a * b) * c = c * c = e$$
$$\therefore \qquad a * (b * c) = (a * b) * c$$

III. That e is an identity element for the above system follows immediately from the first row and first column of the above table.

IV. That each of the elements e, a, b and c has an inverse, immediately follows from the fact that the identity element e occurs in every row of the table.

EXERCISES 5.1

1. Show that the set of all even integers under the operation of addition is a group.

2. Is the set of all odd integers under the operation of multiplication a group?

3. Show that the set of all non-singular 2 × 2 matrices under the operation of matrix multiplication is a group.

4. Show that the set of all subsets of some universal set under the operation ∪ is not a group.

5. Show that the set K whose elements are the matrices

$$I = \begin{bmatrix} 1 & 0 \\ 0 & 1 \end{bmatrix}, \quad A = \begin{bmatrix} -1 & 0 \\ 0 & -1 \end{bmatrix}, \quad B = \begin{bmatrix} 1 & 0 \\ 0 & -1 \end{bmatrix}, \quad C = \begin{bmatrix} -1 & 0 \\ 0 & 1 \end{bmatrix}$$

is a group under the operation of matrix multiplication.

What is the identity element? What is the inverse of the element B?

6. Complete the following group 'multiplication' table

*	I	A	B	C
I	I	A	B	C
A	A			I
B	B		I	
C	C	I		

Simplify A * (B * C), (A * B) * (B * C). What elements are their own inverses?

7. Consider the equilateral triangle ABC as given in the following diagram.

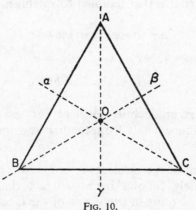

FIG. 10.

As elements of a set take the following rotations of the triangle into itself:

I = identity element, i.e. no rotation.

L = anti-clockwise rotation in the plane of $\triangle ABC$ about the point 0 through 120°.

M = anti-clockwise rotation in the plane of $\triangle ABC$ about the point 0 through 240°.

X = rotation in space about the line α through 180°.

Y = rotation in space about the line β through 180°.

Z = rotation in space about the line γ through 180°.

We shall say that two rotations are equal if the final vertex positions of $\triangle ABC$ are identical and by L * M we shall mean the rotation M acting on $\triangle ABC$ followed by the rotation L acting on $\triangle ABC$. Thus for example L * Z changes

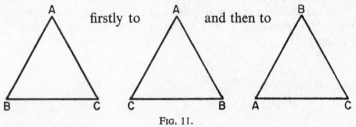

FIG. 11.

and hence L * Z = X.

Construct the group multiplication table for this set of elements under the operation *. Verify that M * (X * Y) = (M * X) * Y. What are the inverses of L and Z?

8. Consider the square ABCD as given in the following diagram.

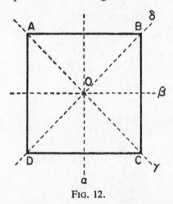

FIG. 12.

As elements of a set take the following rotations of the square into itself:

I = identity element, i.e. no rotation.

L = anti-clockwise rotation in the plane of the square about the point 0 through 90°.

M = anti-clockwise rotation in the plane of the square about the point 0 through 180°.

N = anti-clockwise rotation in the plane of the square about the point 0 through 270°.

P = rotation in space about the line α through 180°.

Q = rotation in space about the line β through 180°.

R = rotation in space about the line γ through 180°.

S = rotation in space about the line δ through 180°.

As in the previous exercise we shall mean by L * M, for example, the rotation M acting on the square followed by the rotation L acting on the square.

Construct the group multiplication table for this set of elements under the operation *. Is it Abelian? What are the inverses of L, M and N?

ANSWERS TO EXERCISES

EXERCISES 1.2 (page 2)

1. (a) $-5, 5$ (d) $2, 4, 6, 8, \ldots$
    (b) $-\frac{2}{3}, -\frac{3}{2}$ (e) 3
    (c) 1   (f) $4, 6, 8, 9, 10, 12, 14, 15, 16, \ldots$

EXERCISES 1.3 (page 3)

1.   (a) True   (c) False
         (b) False   (d) True

2.   (a) True   (d) False
         (b) True   (e) True
         (c) True   (f) False

EXERCISES 1.5 (page 6)

1. (a) $\{3, 4, 5, 6, 7, 8, 9, 11\}$ (e) $\{2, 3, 4, 5, 6, 7, 8, 9, 10, 11\}$
   (b) $\{4, 6, 8\}$ (f) $\{2, 3, 4, 5, 6, 7, 8, 9, 10, 11\}$
   (c) $\{2, 4, 6, 8, 10\}$ (g) $\{9, 11\}$
   (d) $\{3, 5, 7\}$ (h) $\{3, 5, 7\}$

2. (a) The set of all mathematicians who speak either English or German (or both).
   (b) The set of all mathematicians who speak both Russian and German.
   (c) The set of all mathematicians who speak Russian and who do not speak English.
   (d) The set of all mathematicians who either speak English or do not speak German (or both).
   (e) The set of all mathematicians who do not speak both English and Russian.
   (f) The set of all mathematicians who either speak English or both German and Russian.
   (g) The set of all mathematicians who speak German and either do not speak English or Russian.

3.   (a) $A \cap M$ (c) $E \cap M$
           (b) $A \cap E'$ (d) $A' \cap E$
               (e) $M \cup E'$

4. $P(A) = \{\{a, b, c\}, \{a, b\}, \{a, c\}, \{b, c\}, \{a\}, \{b\}, \{c\}, \phi\}$
        $P(B) = \{\{b, c, d\}, \{b, c\}, \{b, d\}, \{c, d\}, \{b\}, \{c\}, \{d\}, \phi\}$
     $P(A \cap B) = \{\{b, c\}, \{b\}, \{c\}, \phi\}$

EXERCISES 1.6 (page 8)

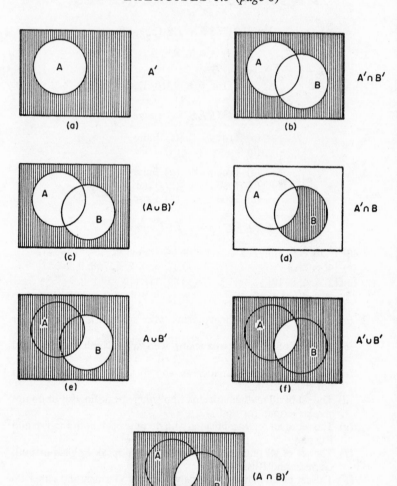

$$\text{I } A' \cap B' = (A \cup B)'$$
$$\text{II } A' \cup B' = (A \cap B)'$$

2.

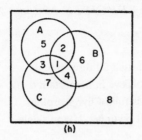

(h)

(a) $A \cap B \cap C$ is region marked 1 in the diagram
(b) $A \cap B \cap C'$ is region marked 2 in the diagram
(c) $A \cap B' \cap C$ is region marked 3 in the diagram
(d) $A' \cap B \cap C$ is region marked 4 in the diagram
(e) $A \cap B' \cap C'$ is region marked 5 in the diagram
(f) $A' \cap B \cap C'$ is region marked 6 in the diagram
(g) $A' \cap B' \cap C$ is region marked 7 in the diagram
(h) $A' \cap B' \cap C'$ is region marked 8 in the diagram

It follows that

$$(A \cap B \cap C) \cup (A \cap B \cap C') \cup (A \cap B' \cap C) \cup (A' \cap B \cap C) \cup (A \cap B' \cap C') \cup$$
$$(A' \cap B \cap C') \cup (A' \cap B' \cap C) \cup (A' \cap B' \cap C') = \mathscr{E}.$$

EXERCISES 1.8 (page 14)

1.   (a) $A \cap B$ (d) $A \cap C'$
     (b) $\mathscr{E}$ (e) $(A \cap B) \cup (A \cap C)$
     (c) $B \cap C$ (f) A

2.   (a) X   (d) Y
          (b) ϕ (e) $X \cup Y$
          (c) X   (f) Y

3.   (a) B'   (d) $A' \cap B$
     (b) $\mathscr{E}$ (e) $A \cup B'$
     (c) $(A \cap B') \cup (A' \cap B)$ (f) $B' \cup D' \cup (A \cap C)$

4. $(A \cup B) \cap (A' \cup C) \cap (B \cup C) = (A \cup B) \cap (A' \cup C)$

5. $(A \cap B) \cup (C \cap D' \cap E) \cup (B' \cap C \cap D')$

The dual result is

$$(A \cup B) \cap (A' \cup C \cup D' \cup E) \cap (B' \cup C \cup D')$$
$$= (A \cup B) \cap (C \cup D' \cup E) \cap (B' \cup C \cup D')$$

EXERCISES 1.9 (page 20)

1. No.
2. No.
3. 3 housewives had used all three brands.
4. Mathematicians believe in immortality.
5. My writing desk is full of live scorpions.
6. Each person must be under 21 and single.

EXERCISES 2.1 (page 22)

1.
(a) Yes	(e) Yes
(b) No	(f) Yes
(c) Yes	(g) Yes
(d) Yes	

EXERCISES 3.2 (page 26)

1. (a), (c), (d), (f) and (h) are propositions.
2. (a) Some students are not industrious.
   (b) One side of Mercury does not always face the Sun.
   (c) Either I do not like eating plums or I do not like drinking lemonade.
   (d) A power of 2 sometimes ends in a 7.
   (e) The sun will not be shining and I shall not carry my umbrella.

EXERCISES 3.4 (page 31)

1. (a) High-speed driving is dangerous and Confucius was a wise man.
   (b) High-speed driving is not dangerous or Confucius was a wise man.
   (c) High-speed driving is not dangerous and Confucius was not a wise man.
   (d) High-speed driving is dangerous and Confucius was a wise man or high-speed driving is not dangerous and Confucius was not a wise man.
   (e) Either high-speed driving is dangerous or Confucius was a wise man, but not both.

EXERCISES 3.5 (page 33)

1. (a) $p' \wedge q'$ (b) F

(c) T   (d) p'

(e) $r \vee p'$ (f) $(p \wedge q) \vee (q' \wedge r)$

(g) $p \wedge q' \wedge r' \wedge s'$

EXERCISES 3.6 (page 37)

2. (a) $p \wedge q'$ (b) $(p \wedge q') \vee (p' \wedge q)$

4. (a) $p \rightarrow q$ (b) $q \rightarrow p$

  (c) $p \rightarrow q$ (d) $p' \leftrightarrow q'$

EXERCISES 4.2 (page 43)

1. $A + B = \begin{bmatrix} 5 & -2 \\ -1 & 8 \end{bmatrix}$ $A - B = \begin{bmatrix} 1 & 0 \\ 1 & 2 \end{bmatrix}$

   $3A + 2B = \begin{bmatrix} 13 & -5 \\ -2 & 21 \end{bmatrix}$ $A - 4B = \begin{bmatrix} -5 & 3 \\ 4 & -7 \end{bmatrix}$

2. $A + B = \begin{bmatrix} 1 & -1 & 2 \\ 9 & 16 & -1 \\ 9 & 0 & 6 \end{bmatrix}$ $B - A = \begin{bmatrix} -1 & 1 & -4 \\ 5 & 6 & 1 \\ 1 & -6 & 2 \end{bmatrix}$

   $5A - B = \begin{bmatrix} 5 & -5 & 16 \\ 3 & 14 & -5 \\ 15 & 18 & 6 \end{bmatrix}$ $2A + 3B = \begin{bmatrix} 2 & -2 & 3 \\ 25 & 43 & -2 \\ 23 & -3 & 16 \end{bmatrix}$

3. $3A - 2B + C = \begin{bmatrix} -2 - 10i \\ 6 + i \\ 8 + 10i \\ 10 + 9i \end{bmatrix}$

EXERCISES 4.4 (page 47)

2. $A = \frac{1}{2}(A + A') + \frac{1}{2}(A - A')$

3. $B = \begin{bmatrix} 3 & 3 & 6 \\ 3 & 3 & 4 \\ 6 & 4 & 9 \end{bmatrix}$ $C = \begin{bmatrix} 0 & -2 & -1 \\ 2 & 0 & 3 \\ 1 & -3 & 0 \end{bmatrix}$

EXERCISES 4.5 (page 52)

1. $AB = \begin{bmatrix} 3 & -2 & -12 \\ 11 & 11 & -5 \\ -1 & -8 & 10 \end{bmatrix}$ $BA = \begin{bmatrix} 13 & 3 & -18 \\ -8 & 6 & 2 \\ -2 & 9 & 5 \end{bmatrix}$

   $A(BA) = (AB)A = \begin{bmatrix} -22 & 9 & 1 \\ -21 & 33 & 38 \\ 28 & -3 & -41 \end{bmatrix}$

2.   I
$$\begin{bmatrix} 3 & 3 \\ 3 & 5 \\ 6 & 8 \end{bmatrix}$$
II [30]

III
$$\begin{bmatrix} 1 & 2 & 3 & 4 \\ 2 & 4 & 6 & 8 \\ 3 & 6 & 9 & 12 \\ 4 & 8 & 12 & 16 \end{bmatrix}$$
IV [5   −3   5]

3.
$$(A + I_3)(A - I_3) = \begin{bmatrix} 20 & 1 & -1 \\ 0 & 11 & 9 \\ 0 & 3 & 17 \end{bmatrix}$$

EXERCISES 4.6 (page 53)

5.

$(A - B)^2 = A^2 - AB - BA + B^2$

$(A - B)^3 = A^3 - A^2B - ABA - BA^2 + AB^2 + BAB + B^2A - B^3$

If matrices commute then

$$(A - B)^2 = A^2 - 2AB + B^2$$
$$(A - B)^3 = A^3 - 3A^2B + 3AB^2 - B^3$$

6.   I 2(BA − AB)

          II 2B(AB + BA)

7. 0

EXERCISES 4.8 (page 57)

1.
$$\left. \begin{aligned} y_1 &= -11u_1 + 18u_2 \\ y_2 &= 27u_1 - 4u_2 \end{aligned} \right\}$$

2.
$$\left. \begin{aligned} y_1 &= -49v_1 + 19v_2 \\ y_2 &= -14v_1 + 18v_2 \end{aligned} \right\}$$

EXERCISES 4.10 (page 63)

3. $(a^2 + b^2 + c^2 + d^2)(x^2 + y^2 + u^2 + v^2)$
$$= (ax + by - cu + dv)^2 + (ay - bx + cv + du)^2$$
$$+ (au + bv + cx - dy)^2 + (av - bu - cy - dx)^2$$

EXERCISES 4.12 (page 68)

1. I $\dfrac{1}{7} \begin{bmatrix} 4 & -3 \\ 1 & 1 \end{bmatrix}$

II $\dfrac{1}{31} \begin{bmatrix} 5 & 4 \\ \dfrac{}{x} & \dfrac{}{x} \\ \dfrac{-4}{y} & \dfrac{3}{y} \end{bmatrix}$

III $\dfrac{1}{83} \begin{bmatrix} 17 & 6 & -8 \\ -21 & 17 & 5 \\ 33 & -3 & 4 \end{bmatrix}$

IV $\dfrac{1}{88} \begin{bmatrix} 16 & -8 & 16 \\ -10 & 38 & -32 \\ -7 & 9 & 4 \end{bmatrix}$

2. $x = 1, \quad y = -1, \quad z = -1$

3. $A^{-1} = \tfrac{1}{5} \begin{bmatrix} -1 & 9 & -3 \\ -2 & 3 & -1 \\ 2 & -13 & 6 \end{bmatrix}$

Hence
$$x = \tfrac{1}{5}(-a + 9b - 3c)$$
$$y = \tfrac{1}{5}(-2a + 3b - c)$$
$$z = \tfrac{1}{5}(2a + 13b + 6c)$$

EXERCISES 4.13 (page 69)

3. $A^{-1} = \begin{bmatrix} \dfrac{1}{3} & \dfrac{14}{15} & \dfrac{2}{15} \\ \dfrac{2}{3} & \dfrac{-1}{3} & \dfrac{2}{3} \\ \dfrac{-2}{3} & \dfrac{2}{15} & \dfrac{11}{15} \end{bmatrix}$

EXERCISES 5.1 (page 74)

2. No.

5. The identity element is I and the inverse of B is B.

6.

$*$	I	A	B	C
I	I	A	B	C
A	A	B	C	I
B	B	C	I	A
C	C	I	A	B

$A * (B * C) = B$ and $(A * B) * (B * C) = I$.

I and B are their own inverses.

7.

*	I	L	M	X	Y	Z
I	I	L	M	X	Y	Z
L	L	M	I	Y	Z	X
M	M	I	L	Z	X	Y
X	X	Z	Y	I	M	L
Y	Y	X	Z	L	I	M
Z	Z	Y	X	M	L	I

The inverses of L and Z are M and Z respectively.

8.

*	I	L	M	N	P	Q	R	S
I	I	L	M	N	P	Q	R	S
L	L	M	N	I	R	S	Q	P
M	M	N	I	L	Q	P	S	R
N	N	I	L	M	S	R	P	Q
P	P	S	Q	R	I	M	N	L
Q	Q	R	P	S	M	I	L	N
R	R	P	S	Q	L	N	I	M
S	S	Q	R	P	N	L	M	I

The group is not Abelian. The inverses of L, M, N are N, M and L respectively.

INDEX